INTRODUCTION: THE POWER

For legal purposes Alan John cannot guarantee suggestions of the content, as well as guarantee permitted by the law, Alan John shall not be responsible for any loss due to the usage of the information in this book, eBook, or any reproduction in any form. All images are original property of the author or copyright-free as stated by image sources. Names of companies and people do not necessarily reflect real-life names or titles. By reading beyond this page and putting into action anything recommended in this book, you hereby consent to this disclaimer and agree to its terms.

Copyright © 2020 by Alan W. John

All rights reserved. This book or parts thereof may not be reproduced in any form, stored in any retrieval system, or transmitted in any form by any means – electronic, mechanical, photocopy, recording, or otherwise – without prior written permission of the publisher, except for the use of brief quotations under the United States copyright law. For permission requests, contact tradingforteens@gmail.com

Alan John, 2020

Contact tradingforteens@gmail.com for further information regarding copyright, fair use, or this disclaimer.

Dedicated to all those who strive to be better, to push the limits, to improve themselves and improve the world.

Thank you.

Table of Contents

Introduction: The Power of Investing 6

Part 1: Benefits 8

Part 2: Getting Stared 12

    Opening an Actual Account 13

    Making Your First Investment 16

    Make Money as a Teen: The Top 5 Businesses 17

    Saving Money as a Teen: The Top 3 Tips 35

Part III: Stock Market Literacy 40

    Basic Terms 41

    Types of Stocks 52

    Types of Investments 60

    How to Understand the Fundamentals 64

    Understanding Earnings 69

Part IV: Stock Market Strategy for Teenagers 75

    What to do When Everything's Going Down 82

    The Rule of Opposites 85

    Understanding the Economy 87

    Cutting Losses 88

    Don't Be Emotional 88

    Diversify 89

    Prices Don't Matter 89

    Trade What You Know 91

    Buy Damaged Stocks, Not Damaged Companies 92

    No Woulda, Shoulda, Coulda 93

Part V: In Practice *94*

    Real-Life Examples 95

    From The Experts 103

    Warren Buffet 104

    Benjamin Graham 105

    Seth Klarman 106

    Sir John Templeton 107

    Thomas Rowe Price, Jr 108

    Bill Ackman 109

    Bill Miller 110

    John Neff 111

    Jesse Livermore 112

    Peter Lynch 113

    John C. "Jack" Bogle 114

Conclusion: You Made It! *116*

Part VI: Resources and Further Information *117*

    Websites: 118

    Books: 119

    YouTube Channels: 123

    Podcasts: 124

    Reselling Apps: 125

Introduction: The Power of Investing

Right now, as you're reading this, you're giving yourself an advantage. Learning how to invest in the stock market, as well as learning about the related skills of money management and financial literacy, is truly valuable. The knowledge in this book can change your financial horizon, as well as expose you to numerous opportunities which otherwise wouldn't be enjoyed. It all begins here. Sit down, grab a snack, and read on.

Investing in all forms is a great way to make money and to plant the seeds to a financially secure future. As a teenager, the skills and habits that you develop will last for life, and it's instrumental that you develop these skills and habits as soon as you can. I wrote this book because as a teenager, (yup, me too) investing has always been a source of passion, not to mention enjoying the financial benefits. No matter your age, no matter the amount of money available to you, you can invest if you choose to, and I hope that this guide will help you do just that and do it successfully. This book is intended to prepare you to have success in the stock market, with the encompassing mission being to ensure the financial freedom of its readers. Throughout the following six sections, you will learn how to earn and save money (with the goal of investing that money), how to open an actual account to start trading and how to understand all the terms, charts, and stats surrounding stocks. At the end, you will see some real-life trades that exemplify the lessons and theories discussed in this book, as well as learn from some of the most successful traders in history. Most people aren't exposed to this information at your age, so be careful with it. Treat it with care and understand its importance. Most importantly, use it. It's truly powerful and can change your life if you put in the time and the work. Without further ado, let's jump into Part 1.

Part 1: Benefits

We need to examine some of the benefits that come as a result of investing at an early age to lay the groundwork for understanding not just how to do it, but why we do it. If you're a teen with parents against you investing, or vice versa, show this section to the opposing party. Later in the book, you'll learn how to develop the necessary skills with no risk and no investment, and that's a great option if you're concerned about the risk.

Investing at an early age yields two categories of benefits: the knowledge and experience that comes from investing and the financial benefits that can come from years of profit and compound interest. We'll first examine the skills that investing will build.

In a video by the entrepreneur and CEO Sam Ovens called *How Billionaires Think: Decoding the Billionaire Mind*, he questions what makes successful people of any field different from their not-as-successful peers through this paradoxical situation:[1] If a business idea or strategy is given to 100 people with no prior knowledge of the information, the results yield a wide spread. Why can some people take information and create something successful, and others fall flat on their faces? Success, in any form, ultimately comes down to the mind. Developing the right mental discipline, control, and skills are instrumental in shaping a young person's

---

[1] We'll define success as the ability to achieve one's aims.

future. Investing will develop not just long-term adequacy in investing (resulting in greater wealth over a lifetime), but also better emotional control, money-management skills, and a maturity that comes with responsibility. Investing young leads to financial literacy, which in turn helps in all areas of money management. Reading stock charts and analyzing companies will become second nature, and if done right, profitable. The effects of exponential growth and compound interest can be harnessed to create a massive nest egg and consistent income during retirement, as well as reducing the need for a time equals money relationship. In fact, money's ability to grow exponentially is one of the most important reasons to start investing young, if not the most important. This idea, referred to as "compound growth" or "compound interest" needs to be taught to younger generations because the younger a person is, the greater effect compounding of investments can have.

Said simply, money, when invested, creates a snowball effect and money in smart investments increases exponentially over time. Think of the fact that a penny doubled each day for a month becomes worth $10,737,418,24.[2] Real-life exponential growth relies on the same basic principle; in more realistic terms, think of it this way: if you're sixteen and you invest one dollar in the stock market, that dollar will be worth (based on the average stock market returns over the last decade) an astounding $88 by the time the average person retires at age 62.[3] In fact, a dollar will

---

[2] Assuming a 30-day month.
[3] Based on a 2018 survey conducted by Gallup.

double in value (become worth $2 in the stock market) around every 7 years. When you look at it that way, it's essential to get started investing as soon as possible, because every dollar invested as a teen isn't actually worth a dollar in its eventual use to you, but rather much more. That said, you still need to be safe with your money and compound interest won't work if money is squandered. Investing, in any form, is never a get rich quick scheme. The process can be automated and outsourced, but work is always required. Below is a chart that displays the amount of money you would earn at an historically average 10% growth rate (the average over the last century for the S&P 500) by investing in stocks with $100 (year 0 being $100).

Year 1	$110
Year 2	$121
Year 3	$133
Year 4	$146
Year 5	$161
Year 6	$177
Year 7	$195
Year 8	$215
Year 9	$237
Year 10	$261
Year 15	$420
Year 20	$673
Year 25	$1,083
Year 30	$1,745
Year 35	$2,810
Year 40	$4,526

Year 45	$7,289
Year 50	$11,739
Year 100	$1,378,061

While starting, ideas such as compound interest can sound vague, and the process can sound intimidating. With compound interest, (as well as investing in general) the profits get exponentially bigger; therefore, the least profits are made in the first couple of years, so be patient. On top of that, the strength of the economy can enormously impact your results. Despite the seemingly negative impact, these factors force you to follow a disciplined route to investing. You must think long term, a very valuable tool. You will have to learn to control the desire to buy and sell based on emotion and resist the emotional drain caused by the ups and downs of stocks. Learning to control fear and evaluate options builds self-control that applies to all areas of life, from school to a career to investing.

Despite the talk of work, investing can, and should, be fun. You can make your own money. You can be sitting in a classroom, taking a test, and walk out richer than when you walked in. You have control over your finances and have the opportunity to build massive wealth. Make sure to keep it as fun as possible while still taking a disciplined approach so you can keep the longevity of your portfolio alive.

Now, we understand some of the benefits of investing at an early age. Hopefully, you're fired up and ready to start. That's perfect because we're moving onto Part II: Getting Started.

Part 2: Getting Stared

Now that you understand the benefits of investing from an early age and (this is required) you have the backing of a guardian, it's time to learn how to get started trading as a teen. Before starting and trading for real, several precautionary steps should be taken to lessen the risk of losing money and to provide needed education to avoid learning the hard way.

Before signing up to any investment platform or spending a dime, you need to understand the #1 most important step to getting started and staying successful while trading. That step is learning. At this stage in your life, you have time. You don't need to jump in right now. It's much better to take at least a couple of weeks or longer to learn as much as you can about investing. Check out books from the library (a resource section including recommended books will be included), watch tutorials, and read news about the market. Watch the investing shows *Mad Money* and *Squawk on the Street*. Experts like Jim Cramer recommend investors to spend one hour per week researching each stock that they own or want to invest in, so continuous learning is a lifelong process for even the best of investors. On top of all that, make sure to have a decent understanding of the stock market literacy section later in this book. Learning as much as possible will save you money down the line and is instrumental in choosing good stocks and making money.

The next step to be put into action, either during your learning period or afterwards, is to open a virtual portfolio. Virtual portfolios are portfolios that allow you to invest virtual money in real stocks at real market values. The website I use is called HTMW. HTMW, standing for How The Market Works, offers first-time users either $500,000 or $1,000,000 virtual dollars and allows investments in thousands of real-time stocks. HTMW also offers competitions where the best traders can win real money by having the best returns in their virtual portfolios. You can visit them at htmw.com. Investing virtual money in real stocks allows you to learn about the market and how to choose good stocks without the risk of real money. Most people go into investing thinking they're smarter than other people (I'm no exception), and that they'll make money and pick better stocks than everyone else. Managing a virtual portfolio can be an eye-opening experience, as well as allowing you to practice the research and investment processes. Tip: If you open a virtual account, try not to invest all your money in the first week (I speak from experience). Be strategic and wait for great opportunities instead of good ones.

Opening an Actual Account

Once you've learned as much as you can and you understand the basics of investing and picking stocks, it's time to open an actual investment account so you can start trading for real. Opening an account is more difficult for minors than adults and requires the assistance of a guardian. Accounts for minors are called custodial accounts. These accounts allow the minor to legally trade (instead of just trading under the parent's name) and have several benefits. Custodial accounts are taxed at a lower rate, even 0% on much of the initial gains, instead of the usual adult rates (this varies by case.) Custodial accounts automatically transfer ownership to the minor once they reach a certain age, either 18 or 21. Many platforms offer custodial accounts and in this section the pros and cons of the best programs will be discussed.

E*TRADE - etrade.com

E*TRADE is one of the oldest online brokers, with a long history that spans from 1982 to the present. E*TRADE is the platform that I started with and currently use, and offers mutual funds, stocks, and options for $0 commissions along with a full range of research and analyst tools. Custodial users get their own login.

Charles Schwab - schwab.com

Charles Schwab is one of the largest investment firms in the world and offers $0 commission trades along with a wide range of research tools. They offer custodial accounts that use the same login as an existing guardian's account. That said, if your guardian uses this service and doesn't want you to be aware of their financial situation (assuming they also use Charles Schwab), this platform is not for you. If that doesn't apply to you, Charles Schwab is one of the best all-around options.

Stockpile – stockpile.com

Stockpile is an investment platform designed specifically for kids and teens. It offers custodial accounts on a simple and youth-friendly interface in which users can buy fractional shares in large companies. Unfortunately, Stockpile only offers 1000 or so of the largest American companies instead of the full market, and fees are 99-cents per trade. Stockpile has introductory lessons on investing and allows for stock "wish lists" to be sent. Overall, it's a decent option for someone looking for a simplified option. An almost identical platform is Loved at loved.com

TD Ameritrade - tdameritrade.com

TD Ameritrade is a platform that's designed for users with experience and offers access to some of the best research tools on the market. Custodial accounts take $0 commissions and have offer custodial accounts with a focus on saving for college.

Fidelity - fidelity.com

Fidelity's platform offers a full range of research tools along with available investment analysis from experts in the field. Fidelity offers custodial accounts with $0 commissions, no fees, and no minimum balance. Overall, Fidelity is an all-around decent choice for active investors.

Vanguard - vanguard.com

Vanguard is one of the largest brokerage services in the world and offers custodial accounts with $0 commissions and no fees. Vanguard's focus and specialty are Mutual Funds and ETFs, which make the platform better suited for long-term and dividend investors.

Making Your First Investment

At this point, you should have decided which platform you want to invest with. With your parent's assistance, you can start the process of opening an account. You're ready to start investing real money into the real market and to do that, you need money itself. Try to gather at least a couple hundred dollars to start, but much more importantly try to consistently add money. Remember the lesson on compound interest in the benefits section, and keep in mind that every dollar you invest today will be worth exponentially more in the future. To help you out if you're looking for some extra money to invest, let's go over 5 of the best ways to make money as a teenager, all of which I can personally vouch for.

You might be asking yourself: Why so much talk of making money, and soon saving money, while this is a book about investing? Well, money and stock market investing are intertwined. Ensuring success in the stock market starts with making and managing money. Additionally, moneymaking and money-managing skills are important to ensure life-long financial freedom. Without further ado, let's make some money!

Make Money as a Teen: The Top 5 Businesses

Make Money #1: Reselling

No teen business guide would be complete without reselling. As my personal favorite, I've found reselling to be the easiest way to make money, starting with no money or very little money. I used to resell to the tune of $500-$1000 a month (sold, not profited) for years. Beyond the money, I find reselling to be an enjoyable venture because the process and products are varied. Let's dive into what reselling is, the art of the flip, how you can get started today with $0, and an option for those looking to quickly scale their business.

Reselling is basically buying things and selling them for more than you paid. With the Internet, you can resell almost anything, as well as reach hundreds of millions of consumers all from a computer or mobile device.

To resell, you must first find items that can later be sold for a profit. It's best to buy from your community because local sellers usually aren't focused on their profit; instead, an emphasis is placed on getting rid of whatever they're selling. (Think a busy mom trying to fit in spring cleaning.) To buy local, check out the following apps:

- Nextdoor – nextdoor.com
- OfferUp – offerup.com
- 5miles – 5miles.com

- VarageSale – varagesale.com
- Craigslist – craigslist.com
- Mercari – mercari.com

Combined, these apps provide an extremely thorough database of everything being sold in your community. If you're starting out with $0, stay alert for curb alerts or for anything being given away for free. Nextdoor, in my experience, is the best place to do this. While on the apps, make sure to be on the lookout for garage sales and estate sales as well as sales of individual items. Another great place to find inventory is in thrift stores. Goodwill, Salvation Army, and local thrift stores can be great places to buy underpriced items.

If you're not sure what will sell and what won't, go to eBay. Search for an item (or use the picture search feature), then go to filters and set "Sold Items." This will show not what an item is listed for, but the price people are historically willing to pay for it. Then, check the date of the sold items. You want to buy items that sell consistently; aim for one per day. This will ensure there's enough market demand to meet your supply.

With all the resources mentioned above, finding inventory to sell shouldn't be a problem. The next part of the reselling process is to sell. There are two ways to sell: offline and online. Selling online, such as through eBay, is great for niche items that appeal to only a small group of people. Since those people probably aren't likely to be located close to you, online sites provide a great way to reach those customers. However, eBay and any similar websites take about a 20% cut (once PayPal fees are thrown in) of the listing value. Although users under 18 can't legally use eBay (or PayPal), eBay lets users under 18 use an adult's account with the account holder's permission. Selling offline, through the apps mentioned above is better because it increases the profit by 20% in comparison to selling online and saves time otherwise spent packaging and shipping boxes. Selling offline is better for items that appeal to a large audience and are likely to sell in your community.

Listing On eBay

Here are some quick tips to help your eBay listings sell faster.

1. **Optimize the Title, Subtitle and Description**

    In the title, clearly display the name of your item as well as one or two highlights, such as "Brand New" or "Original Packaging." Use the subtitle to elaborate upon a highlight. Use the description to thoroughly explain the item and make sure to mention any damage as well as any positive features. I always like to end the description with a variation of the following sentence: "Please let me know if you have any questions or concerns. Thanks!" Then write your name. Doing this will add personality and help the buyer connect to the item they're buying, thus increasing the likelihood of a sale and the likelihood of receiving a positive review.

2. **Price**

> 90% of my listings use Buy Now instead of Auctions. Make sure never to use Auctions unless the item you're selling is in high demand and you're sure a bidding war will occur. As for price, make sure you have the lowest (within reason) price for niche items with smaller audiences, and for items with high demand that sell multiple units a day set the price to be around the average. If you have an item that isn't selling, consider promoting it through eBay. You will only be charged if the item is bought through the promotion and the prices are fair. Make sure to turn on Easy Pricing, which will automatically lower the listing price by 5% every 5 days until an item sells.

3. **Pictures**

> If your item is brand new or unused (original packaging isn't needed to do this) use stock photos from the manufacturer. If not, take your own pictures and make sure to prioritize good lighting.

The problem with eBay, as well as the largest issue facing resellers, lies in scaling the business. Reselling, from finding, listing, and shipping items takes time, and effectively growing a reselling business is hard work. As a solution, I recommend purchasing liquidation lots from liquidation.com. Buying pallets of returned items (without getting too much into the liquidation business) basically allows you to condense buying items locally into buying dozens or hundreds of items online in a single purchase. If you're interested, make sure to do your own research. If done right, it's extremely profitable and much easier to scale than alternatives.

That wraps up reselling for teens. It's truly an amazing business made possible only in recent times by the internet, and without doubt, should be taken advantage of. Next up, all about service businesses.

Make Money #2: Service Businesses

Service businesses are any businesses that involve providing a service to someone else. As a teen, service businesses are the easiest way to make money fast. Common service businesses for teens include washing cars, babysitting, walking dogs, and house/pet sitting. To start a service-based business, you will need only a few basic supplies (such as a bucket and rags for washing cars) and the harder part of the business revolves around finding clients. First, use your neighborhood or apartment as a resource. People who know you are much more likely to buy from you. Some businesses, such as washing cars, simply involve going door-to-door. Others require more trust between the provider and the client, such as a babysitting business or a dog walking business. (Babysitter Tip: Take the Red Cross Babysitter course and get certified; parents love it.) For those businesses, get the word out, start with a few family members, friends, or neighbors, and make them really, really happy customers. As long as you provide great service, word of mouth will likely take care of expanding your client base.

If you're considering starting any of the service businesses mentioned, remember this: the relationship comes first. Keeping your clients happy and doing quality work will enable your business to grow, as well as building skills and a work ethic that last a lifetime. As a last tip, remember that service-based businesses are centered on you. Make sure to dress presentably, show up on time, and be respectful. If you do all these things, you'll be well on your way to making great money.

Make Money #3: Part-time Jobs

Since this is largely self-explanatory and excludes younger teens, I'll only cover it briefly. Getting a part-time job is a great opportunity to create a consistent and reliable income source as well as to get a taste of a typical adult workday. If you do get a job, try and do something you enjoy, because jobs for teenagers (with exceptions) are typically on the monotonous side.

Make Money #4: Freelance

If you have a unique talent or skill, freelancing is likely for you. Due to recently introduced services like Fiverr and Upwork (fiverr.com and upwork.com), you can use your skills to make great money. Whatever your skill is, start cheap and raise your prices as your reputation and number of reviews grow. Remember, just like service businesses, freelancing has a lot to do with you, so make sure to reply in a timely manner and put the customer first. If you do this and build a reputable online persona, freelancing can be a great and fun way to earn money.

Make Money #5: Online Businesses

Ever since the Internet popped into existence (more so in recent years) business opportunities that require nothing but a device and an Internet connection have become increasingly common. As a teenager who's likely grown up around modern technology and naturally become adept, starting an online business is perfect. We'll cover 4 of the top solely online (not part-online, like reselling on eBay) businesses, all of which I've personally had experience with. Keep in mind the following is just an intro to these businesses so more research would be required if you're interested in getting started. All the following businesses require literally $0 to start, making them ideal for a teen starting out with little capital.

Online Business 1: Kindle Direct Publishing (KDP)

It wouldn't be right not to start off the online business list with KDP because this book was created through KDP. Kindle Direct Publishing by Amazon allows anyone, anywhere in the world to sign up for free and upload documents that are then listed for sale on Amazon and Kindle. When someone buys the book, Amazon prints and ships it for you, and then a portion of the list price goes directly to your bank account. This business model, called print-on-demand, requires no overhead and no investment, making it perfect for someone looking to make money from nothing or from a small investment. It's what allowed this book to reach six-figure sales in under a year completely through word-of-mouth.

Said simply, the strategy I use is to take a topic I know well (you don't have to be an amazing writer to do this, although it's preferred), and then write a short but extremely descriptive and thorough non-fiction book on the subject. To start, just open a Google or Word document and start writing about anything of which you're extremely knowledgeable. If you don't feel you know enough about a topic to write about it, choose something you're passionate about and do a ton of research. Once you've written your book (tip: a good book look has Garamond font, size 11 font and 1.15 inch spacing), sign up for KDP at kdp.com (you may sign up using an Amazon account) and upload it. Then, use professional software, photopea.com (as a free alternative), or Amazon's free Cover Creator software (used while publishing a book on kdp.com) to design a cover. Afterword, just set a price and release your work to the world. Of course, your book likely won't magically blow up, but if you promote your book and/or advertise it, you'll begin to rank in Amazon and get more sales. As an alternative to writing a book, you can pay professional writers on Fiverr or Upwork to write a book for you. Just know that the ghostwriter method would require a much larger investment. Overall, KDP is a huge, not to mention unsaturated, opportunity that should be taken advantage of if you have any interest in writing.

Online Business 2: Merch By Amazon (MBA)

Merch By Amazon is an unsaturated online business that appeals mostly to artists, as well as creative people in general. Merch By Amazon uses the same concept as KDP, except with upper-body clothing. Basically, anyone can upload designs, digitally have their designs put on clothing, and then list that clothing on Amazon. When someone purchases the clothing, Amazon does the printing and shipping, and you get a portion of the money delivered straight to your bank account. All you need is great designs that people will buy. If you're not an artist (by the way, if you like making memes, this is for you) just take the knowledge you've gained from doing whatever you're passionate about, figure out what's popular in that space, and then figure out how to apply those trends to designs. Software such as Photoshop is optimal for designing, but free options such as photopea.com are available (the $30 per month investment for Photoshop will likely pay for itself within a couple months.) Unlike KDP, Merch By Amazon requires an application to enter, and less than 10% (likely much less than that) of applicants get accepted. Amazon limits the amount of new creators in order to not flood the marketplace and even if you are accepted you'll likely have to wait 6 months in the digital "line." With that being said, it is possible to get in and if it's something you're interested in, make sure to give it a shot at merch.amazon.com.

Online Business 3: Affiliate Marketing

Affiliate marketing is basically the business of companies paying you to sell their products. When you successfully sell their products to a customer, you earn a commission out of what the customer pays. For example, let's say Company X is selling a weight loss course for $99. You might post about the course and your aunt might sign up using your link. Once she pays $99 to Company X, Company X then pays you $30. The beauty of this system is that Company X is happy because they got a new customer, you're happy because you got paid, and your aunt is happy (hopefully) because she bought a product or service she loves. While affiliate marketing can be scaled through advertising, it's best to keep it simple for someone just starting out. First, sign up for Clickbank at clickbank.com. Clickbank will provide a database of all the affiliate deals companies are currently offering. Then, choose a product or service you believe in and spread the word throughout your community and on social media. If people use your link to sign up, you get paid. Best yet, some offers are for subscriptions, meaning you would get paid every month as long as the customer stays subscribed.

That's just an intro, but the possibilities of affiliate marketing go far beyond the grassroots marketing techniques described. If it's something you enjoy, do your research because there's a lot to learn. This wraps up online business 3 and takes us to the last online business, which, notably, is last because it's the hardest on this list to provide value in the short term, although the long-term benefits are enormous.

Online Business 4: Social Media
Social Media certainly isn't the fastest way to make money and isn't a great idea if you're looking to make money to invest within a couple of months.

It deserves the final spot on this list because I've found it to be the most fun out of any of the other businesses on this list and the long-term financial value can be enormous. There are so many ways to make money with social media, so to save time, I'll only cover the top 3 ways I make money with social media.

The first two ways of making money with social media involve Instagram. I started with Instagram in 2018, and as of 2021, I've grown a personal brand up to having more than 60,000 followers, a total network of 100,000+ followers, and at some points managed accounts with a total of more than 500,000 followers, all the while selling products, accounts, and services. I tell you this to point out the potential of social media as a business and as a tool to reach an audience, especially for those who have grown up around and became adept at social media. To make money with Instagram, you must first have a large and dedicated audience. Here are a few quick tips to help you grow an account:

Growing on Instagram

1. Myths

First, we'll need to crack open the largest Instagram growth myth, and that is the following: It's easy. Today, in an oversaturated market filled with people who are smarter, better looking, harder working, and more talented than you, growing an account is so much more difficult than people think. You may see an account with a hundred thousand followers and think they just got lucky, or posted a video that went viral, and they suddenly got to where they are. However, behind the scenes the creator of that account likely worked for hours, day after day, month after month, to find the best content and optimize it. In my opinion, the results are worth it, but if you don't enjoy it, just don't do it. Later we'll go over a strategy to make money on Instagram that doesn't require growing an account and takes much less time. If you're in, continue reading.

2. Create & Optimize an Account

First, you must create an account. There are two different kinds of accounts you may potentially create: a personal page or a theme page. A personal page is an account that's all about you, and a theme page is focused on a certain topic. For example, I have a personal fitness page, currently at 18k followers, and a theme page about fitness, currently at just over 22k followers. Theme pages are easier to grow because the theme of the page will already have a dedicated audience, while a personal page is difficult to grow unless you have a special talent or you provide something that would make people want to follow you, such as providing educational videos about a topic you specialize in.

Once you've chosen what kind of account you want to start, you need to optimize it. This means you'll need to do everything you can to make the account ready to grow before posting. First, start with the name of the account. For a personal page, use some variation of your name or if the page is focused on something you do, put that in the title (for example: A fitness page for John Doe might be @johndoefitness or @jdlifting). As a theme page, make sure your title conveys exactly the type of content you will provide. For example, a business-related account might name itself @topbusinesstips and @petrabbits might work for an (you guessed it) account about pet rabbits. Once you have named your account, you can move on to the description, commonly known as the bio. All my accounts use a strategy that incorporates emojis and lines to cleanly convey key points about the account. Here's what a bio might look like for @petrabbits. Note: For a theme page, the name input can be used for something other than the creator's name, in this case, "Tips for rabbit owners." A personal page should obviously put their name in the name section.

> Tips for Rabbit owners
> 😊 | Only the best information ☺
> 💧 | A home for rabbit owners
> Follow for daily bunny content!!

You can use this format to optimize your bio and clearly convey the purpose of your account. Next, make sure to change the account to a business or creator account (settings < account < professional account) so that you'll be able to see account insights, which will in turn help you further optimize your account. Once this is done, add a profile picture. Make sure the picture is visually appealing, not too confusing, and is relevant to the purpose of your page. Finally, follow some of the top influencers or theme accounts in your niche and set the account to public. Now that you've completed all these steps, your account is optimized and ready to go.

3. Optimizing your Posting Strategy

Next, you must determine the type of content you'll post and how often you'll post it. A personal page will use content about themselves; a theme page can either design their own content or use other people's content and give credit. Decide what's best for you based on the tools you have access to and the time you're willing to invest in creating your posts. For every post, you'll need a thoughtful description. A description should have a hook at the top (something to catch the reader's attention and keep them engaged), and at least 50% of posts should have a long caption underneath the hook that tells a story or explains a subject. The description doesn't always need to be exactly related to the post. (For example, a fitness influencer might post a picture of them working out and then write about their favorite protein shake in the description.) Finally, use an eye-catching format to ask the follower to engage and add hashtags at the bottom. Here's what a post description might look like for @petrabbits:

> This study proves why your rabbits need a healthy diet :)
> Comment if you think so ☺
> .
> .
> .
> ✔ Make sure to give us a follow for more daily rabbit content
> ✔ If you have any questions let us know
> .
> .
> .

#petrabbit #petrabbits #rabbit #rabbitowner #rabbitowners #rabbittips #rabbittip #rabbitfood #howtoraisearabbit #howtoraiserabbits

Make sure to vary the popularity of hashtags you use (use 20 – 25 per post, 5 should have 1 million+ posts, 10 should be under 500k, and 10 should be under 100k) as well as vary the set of hashtags used, as in, don't use the same 25 hashtags on all your posts. Now that your posts are optimized, you need to know how often you'll post and when. To answer the when, simply check out your insights (insights will only be accurate once an account has been posting consistently for at least a couple of weeks) or google "best times to post on Instagram."

To figure out how often to post, understand this: To grow on Instagram today, you must post a baseline of 1 post per day and at least 3 or 4 stories a day for a personal account and 2 posts per day along with 6 - 7 stories per day for a theme account. Unless you're a celebrity or have some other source of attracting followers, that's the harsh reality. Growing on social media does take a lot of time and work (keep in mind, the results are exponential and are typically slow for the first couple of months), so as I've said before, only do it if you love it.

4. Growth Strategies

Last up are growth strategies. To grow quickly, do as many shoutouts as possible (sfs is a common means of asking for a shoutout and means "Shoutout For Shoutout") with relevant accounts. Comment on other people's posts in your niche, and finally engage users several times a day through stories, specifically questions and polls. Consistently performing these steps will significantly increase your growth. As a final tip, don't ever buy followers or shout-outs that promise followers. (If you're interested in grassroots marketing techniques, make sure to google Gary Vanyerchuck's $1.80 marketing strategy.)

That's all for growing on Instagram. Next up is how to monetize your account and followers. First, sell shoutouts. This can only be done if you have a significant following, but once you do have a following it's an easy source of income. In your bio, add a line that says "DM me for shoutouts" if you want to pursue this strategy.

Since Instagram connects you to a large audience, another great way to make money off an account is to sell to your audience. Affiliate marketing and Clickbank are two easy ways to generate revenue without developing your own product. If you do have your own product or products to sell, go for it. Just remember to not be too "salesy." As a rule, mention your product in 1 out of every 10 posts. Don't forget to add a link in the website section of your bio that directs users to your products.

Those are the two best ways to make money with a large account, but growing an account is hard and there's a much easier method to make money off Instagram, one that doesn't require growing an account. That method is by reselling, or "flipping" Instagram accounts. Remember, anything can be resold, and Instagram accounts are no exception. Using virtual marketplaces, you can buy Instagram accounts for cheap and sell them for more. Here are the 3 best sites to buy and sell Instagram accounts on:

- Socialtradia.com
- Fameswap.com
- Insta-sale.com

Before purchasing an account, make sure the followers aren't fake (check out app.hypeauditor.com and influencermarketinghub.com to perform quality checks) and make sure the account has high engagement. Lastly, always buy through the escrow services of one of the sites mentioned above and never through PayPal, Cash App, or a wire transfer.

That covers the best 2 ways to make money off Instagram (to recap: through growing accounts and flipping accounts) and now let's move on to the third best way to profit off of social media: YouTube.

YouTube

Since I started posting on YouTube in 2018, I've amassed 2500 subscribers and more than 400,000 views, along with an average payout of $7.48 per 1000 monetized views. While I may not have the largest audience, I've been able to make a significant amount of money through ads, merch, and an eBook that's related to the channel. Starting and growing a YouTube channel is an enormous task, and I'll just leave you with a couple of tips. First, make sure you're posting videos about something you love. YouTube requires work and enjoying what you do and finding it meaningful is the only way to prevent burnout and keep the longevity of the channel alive. Second, understand that not everything needs to be perfect when starting out. Shooting on your phone, in your room and without being a good-looking smooth talker is perfectly fine. Fun Fact: I have a video that currently has more than 160,000 views that had my brother, who was 8 at the time, wander on camera and play with slime. I never noticed it while filming or in post-production and as a result 160,000 people have seen my greatest mistake as a content creator.

Next, establish a consistent posting routine. Try and post at least on the same day (per week) and better yet at the same hour, so your audience will start to expect your videos and be ready to watch them. Finally, once you have an established audience, use resources such as Merch By Amazon (merchbyamazon.com) and KDP (kdp.com) to make money through your audience. That's just an intro to growing and making money on YouTube. The topic is huge and if it's something you're interested in you'll need to do your own research.

That wraps up making money with social media, as well as the top 5 businesses that teens can start. If you want specific tips on any of the mentioned businesses, email me at tradingforteens@gmail.com.

Now that you're on your way to making money, you should learn how to effectively manage and save your money so you have more to invest.

Saving Money as a Teen: The Top 3 Tips

Out of Sight, Out of Mind

The first and possibly the most effective money-saving rule is the idea that if money is kept out of sight, it will be seen less and therefore used less. It's easy to buy that chocolate bar or that new sweatshirt while carrying a wallet stuffed with money, and in an increasingly digital world, services like Apple Pay and PayPal grant people easy access to their money from their devices. While this may be useful, technology makes it easy to impulse buy instead of making thoughtful decisions that ultimately reflect your best long-term interests. To counter impulse spending, use the Out of Sight, Out of Mind rule. The goal is to make your money less accessible so you can save and invest more. To start, put cash somewhere that requires effort to get to. Even better, give it to a guardian and then ask them to require you to thoughtfully explain why you want your money. The same rules apply to credit and debit cards. If you currently have normal spending habits, you will see almost instant improvement in the amount of money you're able to save. To learn more about how small purchases impact your finances, check out the books, *The Automatic Millionaire* and *The Millionaire Next Door*. However, cash is becoming less and less common. If you have a phone, you'll need to lock that down as well. Disconnect Apple Pay and Samsung Pay to prevent easy spending from your phone and move money away from PayPal to prevent easy impulse purchases online. To those with a job or a consistent paycheck coming in, automatically send 50% (or as much as you wish) of your income to your stock trading account. This way, by the time you receive your money, you will already have saved a substantial amount of your income. All these tips are great, but at the end of the day you'll likely need to spend some money, such as while spending time with friends or family. The goal of Out of Sight, Out of Mind isn't to completely stop you from spending money; it's to help you spend money only on what really makes you happy and eliminate purchases you would later regret.

Start at the End

A great second step to help you save money is, so to speak, to start at the end. In simpler terms, set goals. Saving money can be hard because it fights the natural desire for short-term gratification. Basically, the motivation isn't there. Having incremental goals and achieving them will release dopamine, just like the short-term gratification that money can buy. Therefore, having a large goal, say to save $1000, and incremental goals, such as to save $50 a week, is an effective way to make saving money fun as well as align it with your brain's natural instincts. To best use this strategy, set up goals that can be reached every week as well as an encompassing end goal. The end goal should take at least several months to complete otherwise it wouldn't feel "worth it." To set up goals, a great method can be found in Peter Drucker's SMART goal system. SMART stands for:

- o Specific
- o Measurable
- o Attainable

- Relevant
- Time-Bound

For example, someone looking to save money could use this as their SMART goal: I want to save $500 in the next 3 months to invest in stocks. I will do this by babysitting for my neighbors and saving the allowance my parents give me. I will break my goal down by saving $50 per week. Here's some space to write your own SMART goal that will help you save money to invest:

Understand I personally invest in market. Aim to turn £200 into £400 minimum. Reinvest profits

I will achieve this goal by: *The end of 2021*

Signed: _____

To learn more about the (I may be biased, but very interesting) world of willpower, motivation, and gratification make sure to check out the following books: *The Willpower Instinct* by Kelly McGonigal and *High-Performance Habits: How Extraordinary People Become That Way* by Brendon Burchard.

Shop Smart

A third rule to help you save money is all about shopping smart. This section isn't about eliminating your shopping habits; it's about helping you save money while shopping by only purchasing items you truly want.

First, sleep on it. As mentioned above, impulse buying can be a huge waste of money. If you're considering purchasing any item of significant value don't immediately purchase it. <u>Take a night to think about it.</u> If you wake up and the item is something you truly think you'll love and will add value and happiness to your life, go ahead and buy it. However, you'll often wake up and be really, really glad you didn't purchase it. This is a great rule for anyone to implement and you'll soon find money piling up.

Second, don't buy new. (There are obvious exceptions to this rule; I'll leave that up to you to decide.) Using resources such as eBay, thrift stores, secondhand stores, and the apps Nextdoor, Letgo, OfferUp, 5miles, Craigslist and VarageSale will often result in products of great quality for a huge discount off retail prices. Take this example: One of the books mentioned in the resources section, *Rich Dad Poor Dad For Teens* by Robert Kiyosaki sells for $13.99 on audible and $9.99 on Target's website. The same book sells (in good condition) for $4.19 on thriftbooks.com and other book resale websites. The same rule holds for clothes, technology, and other products. AirPods, which retail for nearly $150, go for under $100 on sites like Letgo and OfferUp. (Fun fact: I purchased an AirPod case with only 1 AirPod to save money. It cost only $40.) Deals are everywhere if you take the time to look for them.

As a third tip for shopping smart, be aware of timing. The right timing can lead to significant deals and discounts. Take Black Friday. Black Friday is universally known as the day to get the best deals of the year. (If you're in China, replace Black Friday with Singles Day.) Purchasing the new computer you've been saving up for on Black Friday in comparison to the prices of six months later would save you huge amounts of money. While Black Friday is only one day a year, companies offer deals and discounts year-round and knowing when to purchase can help you save big.

If you combine the three tips above, you'll be the smartest shopper on the block, as well as the richest. Use them wisely and make sure to share them with friends and family who (ahem) could improve their spending habits.

Once you've made money, saved money, and you're done learning as much as you can, it's time to get to the hard part: choosing stocks and making money. This concludes Part II and it's time to move into Part III: Stock market literacy.

Part III: Stock Market Literacy

Before learning strategies and methods to make money in the stock market, you must first understand some of the basic terms and words that are used to describe stocks and evaluate them. The first time you see the P/E ratio or the earnings call of a company, you'll likely be overwhelmed, but the following information will set you off on the right foot. You don't need to memorize every word, just try to understand the basic components and beyond that, use this content as a reference guide that can be turned to if a word or concept is not understood later in your investing journey.

Throughout this section, you'll learn about the following:

1. **Basic Terms**
2. **Types of Stocks**
3. **Types of Investments**
4. **How to Understand the Fundamentals**
5. **How to Understand Earnings**

Basic Terms

→ learn it all

To start off, you'll need to learn some words and terms that are at the core of investing. Only the more important words have been included, as all the terms out there could fill a book by themselves.

Stock

A stock is a very small piece of a company that is sold on a public or private market. As the value of a company increases, the value of its stock can also increase.

Stock Market

The stock market comprises public exchanges that allow stocks to be bought and sold. Typically, large countries will have their own stock markets.

Stock Exchange

An exchange is related to the stock market, but while the stock market is an umbrella term, a stock exchange is where the stocks are actually bought and sold. For example, the NYSE is an American stock exchange that allows American companies (along with some international companies) to publicly trade.

Wall Street

Wall Street is the street in New York where US stock exchanges are located. However, the term Wall Street is often used to describe the people who work on Wall Street as well as the market and the market's movements.

Stock Symbol

A stock symbol is typically two to five letters that represent a company's stock. For example, Apple's stock symbol is AAPL, and Amazon's is AMZN.

Sector

Stock Market Sectors represent different branches of the economy that a stock's company operates in. For example, Apple is a technology company, so their sector is technology. There are 11 sectors in the market, all of which will be explained later in the book.

Portfolio

A portfolio is a collection of many investments held by a person or organization. For example, if you own shares of three different companies, your holdings in those companies comprise your portfolio.

Dividend

A dividend is a sum of money that a company will regularly give to shareholders who own their stock. Dividends are typically paid out quarterly (4 times per year). For example, the company Johnson & Johnson might pay out around 2% of the share price, also known as the dividend yield. If you own 100 shares at $200 ($200 x 100 x 2%), you will receive $400 a year in dividends. Dividends are subject to change and don't necessarily stay the same over a long period of time. As a whole, dividend yields average between 1% to 3% and companies with dividends tend to be safer and consistent in their growth. A great dividend strategy is to automatically <u>reinvest dividend money</u>, which results in a position that increases its holdings over time.

IPO *— → New company w/ potential*

The IPO, or initial public offering, is the launch of a stock on the market. For example, the company Lyft (LYFT) opened at $72 per share at its IPO. IPOs only happen once per company when they are first listed on an exchange.

Market Cap

The market cap of a company is found by multiplying the share price by the number of shares. It basically acts as a determination of the value of a company's stock. For example, a company with a stock price of $100 and 1,000,000 shares available for sale would have a $100,000,000 market cap. As a rule (though with notable exceptions, take Tesla), the larger a company is, the safer it is.

Volatility

Volatility is the likelihood of the amount a stock may rise or fall. For example, a stock that goes up 8% one day, down 10% the following day and up 5% the next day is more volatile than a stock that goes up 1% each day. Volatile stocks are usually the riskiest, although they often have the most upside potential.

To "Execute" an Order

Once you place an order to buy or sell a stock, the process of that order being completed is sometimes referred to as being "executed" or as "going through." As a side note, the price you initially bought a stock for is sometimes called the "purchase point" or "point of entry." (Such as, "I entered AMZN at $900.")

Limit Order

A limit order is one way in which a stock can be bought. A limit order allows a buyer to set a price at which they want to buy a stock that is below the current market price. Your order will only be executed when the stock hits that target price or falls below that target price. For example, a limit order might be to buy 10 shares of Abbott Laboratories (ABT) at $80 while ABT is trading at $85. The trade will only execute if you can purchase those 10 shares at exactly $80 or at any number below $80. A smart strategy while buying into a stock is to set a limit order slightly under the current price. For example, if ABT is trading at $80, you might place a limit order at $76. This would be opposed to setting an order at the current price of $80, having the stock fall to $76, and almost immediately losing 5%. Limit orders are the typical order type.

Market Order

A market order is another type of order that you can place to buy a stock. A market order will purchase the stock at the market value, or the current price of the stock. For example, if Abbott Laboratories is trading at $83.45 and a market order is placed, that trade will immediately execute at $83.45. Market orders are riskier than limit orders because you have less control over the purchase point, but they are useful if you want to enter a stock immediately.

Bear Market

A bear market is a market that isn't doing well and is going down. Hearing investors say, "Oh, the bears are back" or anything similar is referring to the people who are selling. It generally represents a negative view of the market and is sometimes referred to as being bearish.

Bull Market

Bulls and a bull market represent the flip side of a bear market. Bullish investors think the market is going to go up and are buying. A bull market is a market that is doing well and most stocks in a bull market are moving up.

Annual Report

Once per year, a company must deliver an annual report that displays the key statistics of their business, such as sales and debt. Annual reports are good indications of how a company is performing. A company's annual report will line up with one of their quarterly reports and can make a huge impact on share price.

Quarter

The market, as well as all companies, follows a financial calendar that includes 4 quarters. A company must report earnings, which are basically a description of how well the company performed over the previous quarter. A company with a December 31st year-end will have the following quarterly schedule: January, February, and March (Q1); April, May, and June (Q2); July, August, and September (Q3); and October, November, and December (Q4). Quarterly earnings make a huge impact on stock price and good earnings, as well as bad, can set the course for the next quarter or year.

Close — UK time?

Markets aren't open to most investors 24/7. The US stock market operates from 9:30 am to 4 pm EST from Monday to Friday and is closed on most major holidays. The market close simply refers to the time the market stops trading for the day.

Day Trading

Day trading is a method of investing. While most investors invest for the long term, day traders trade in and out of stocks on a daily (or even less; such as a per minute) basis. For example, if a day trader thinks a company is going to unveil a new product that will drive their stock price up, that day trader will buy shares. Once the news comes out and that stock moves up 5%, they'll sell the stock. Day trading is riskier than long-term investments and generally makes less money over a long period of time, although it can be lucrative if mastered.

Rally

A rally is a sustained period of growth in the market or stock. While bull markets represent a longer period of time, rallies are usually used in a short-term context. For example, a report showing that unemployment has reached a 50-year low might result in a day-long market rally.

Volume

Volume is the number of times a stock has been traded. For example, Microsoft (MSFT) is traded millions of times a day. A smaller stock like Sorrento Therapeutics (SRNE) might only be traded a couple hundred thousand times a day. Spikes in volume usually indicate a (oftentimes large) change in share price, whether up or down.

Yield

Yield is what percentage of the share price a company hands out in dividends. For example, let's say JNJ's stock is trading at $200. If you own 1 share, you will receive $4 a year in dividends. By dividing 4 by 200, we can find that the dividend yield is 0.02, or 2%. The higher the dividend yield, the better.

Day Order

Every time you set a limit order for a stock, you also need to set the duration during which the order can be executed. Day orders execute over the course of one trading day. Other common durations are "60 days" and "Good Until Date," which refers to a custom date being set.

Analyst Research

Analysts are people whose jobs are to find good investments for their firms. Most investment platforms will have an analyst research page. That page will display all the information and ratings given to a stock by analysts who researched it. While analysts aren't always right (for example, TSLA roughly tripled in three months despite analyst negativity), the information and reports they give are useful to consider. When esteemed and reputable analysts write a report stating they believe a stock will either move up or down, (called "upgrading" or "downgrading") a stock will often move in-sync with the report.

Insider Activity

Most investing platforms will display the insider activity information of stocks. People who work at a company (typically in high-ranking corporate positions) are called insiders. Insider activity displays the purchase history of insiders on the stock of the company they work for. This can be useful information. For example, you might find that the CEO of Company X has registered the purchase of 100,000 shares of his or her company. That type of information can be very useful in determining a good time to buy a stock. However, some insider activity doesn't reflect the insider's knowledge. "Award of Options" and "Exercise of Options" represents insiders either being given shares or forced to sell shares. This is pre-planned and has nothing to do with the insider's current opinion of the company. Purchases and sales of the stock are the only insider activity information that you should pay attention to.

Gross Margin

A company's gross margin is the net sales minus the manufacturing cost of the goods sold. For example, a company might sell 10,000 units worth $1 million. Those 10,000 units were assembled for $400,000 and the employee cost to build the units was $100,000. This means that the Gross Margin, 1,000,000 - 400,000 - 100,000, would be 500,000. Then, to convert it into a percentage, divide that number by the original sales number. 500,000 divided by 1,000,000 results in a gross margin of 0.5, or 50%. Gross Margin doesn't provide a complete view of a company's profits since expenses such as marketing cost are not factored into the Gross Margin. However, generally speaking, the higher the gross margin, the healthier a company is. The gross margin of a healthy company should be at least 20%, although that number varies by industry.

Net Profit Margin

A net profit margin is a step beyond gross margin. Net profit margin reveals the true profitability of a company after all expenses have been paid. To find the net profit margin, use this equation: Net Profit Margin = Net Profit ÷ Sales. For example, a company might have $100,000 in sales. From that $100,000 in sales, the company has a profit after all expenses of $30,000. To find the net profit margin, divide 30,000 by 100,000. The result is 0.3. Then, multiply that number by 100 to get a percentage. 0.3 multiplied by 100 equals 30. Therefore, the net profit margin is 30%. Use the net profit margin to determine the true profit a company is making after all expenses have been paid.

Return On Assets (ROA)

Return on assets indicates the profit of a company in comparison to the value of its assets. To find the ROA, divide the net income by the total assets. For example, let's say you start a lemonade stand business. You bought the table, the sign and all the other equipment for $1000. Then, you made $250. To find your ROA, divide 250 by 1000. The result is 0.25 and a return on assets of 25%. ROA could be useful in the following situation: A company with $1 billion in assets and making $1 million in profit might be in the green with an ROA of .1%, but another company might have $100 million in assets and be making $10 million in profit with an ROA of 10%. The company making 100x the money while using 1/10 the value of assets is likely a better investment. The higher the return on assets, the more effective the company is at making money.

Price/Book Ratio (P/B.

A P/B ratio determines whether a stock is undervalued or overvalued by the market. To find it, divide the price per share by the book value per share. The book value of a stock is the total value of a company's assets minus the liabilities. Generally, investors look for a P/B ratio under 3. P/B ratios under 1 generally mean a stock is very undervalued and potentially a good investment. However, understand that P/B ratios vary per industry, so do your homework before making an investment decision based on a P/B ratio.

Price/Cash Flow Ratio (P/CF)

A P/CF ratio compares a company's market value to its cash flow. To find it (using a simplified equation) divide the share price by the cash flow per share. For example, two companies have a share price of $100. One company has a cash flow of $10 per share, while the other has $30 per share. To find their P/CF ratios, divide 10/100 and 30/100. As a percentage, those two companies would have respective P/CF ratios of 10% and 30%. Extremely high and extremely low P/CF ratios are generally not a good sign, most companies have a P/CF ratio ranging from 10 to 20.

Price/Sales Ratio (P/S)

A P/S ratio compares a company's stock price to its revenue per share. Revenue per share can be found by dividing a market cap by total revenue. For example, a company with a $20 share price and revenue per share of $5 has a P/S ratio of 20/5, or 4. P/S ratios show how much investors are willing to pay per dollar of sales. For example, the previous example would show that investors are willing to pay $4 for every $1 of revenue the company generates. P/S ratios are most useful, like P/CF and P/B ratios, in comparing companies in the same sector. In most sectors, P/S ratios under 1 are excellent, and 1 to 2 is considered good.

Types of Stocks

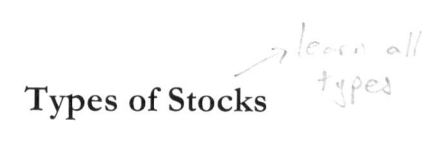

→ learn all types

It's very important to understand different types of stocks. There are many ways to classify a stock, and the most common classifications will be explained. The first common classification of stocks is by the style of investment they represent.

Value Stocks

Value stocks are stocks that are underpriced and undervalued in comparison to other similar companies.

Growth Stocks

Growth stocks belong to companies that are growing quickly or poised to grow quickly. Examples include Amazon and Lyft (AMZN and LYFT).

Cyclical Stocks

Cyclical stocks typically line up with the performance of the market. If the market goes up, cyclical stocks go up. If the market goes down, these stocks are likely to go down with it. Examples include Hasbro and Harley-Davidson. (HAS and HOG).

Penny Stocks

Penny stocks, as the name implies, are low-priced and high-risk investments. They range from $5 to less than 10 cents. Although they're more likely than blue-chip and income stocks to have high upside potential, most are small businesses and are therefore more likely to fail or go bankrupt. Examples include Smith Micro Software and Fortuna Silver Mines (SMSI and FSM).

Speculative Stocks

Speculative stocks are typically small or start-up companies that are new to the stock market and have no track record. They often have new products or are exploring a new market. Speculative stocks are very risky but often have greater upside potential than large and stable stocks. Examples include Fortress Biotech and Sorrento Therapeutics (FBIO and SRNE).

Blue Chip Stocks

Blue-chip stocks are from large, consistently profitable, and well-established companies at the pinnacle of their industries. They generally grow slowly but are low-risk and usually safe. Companies like this include Johnson & Johnson (JNJ) and Apple (AAPL).

Income Stocks

Income stocks are often also blue-chip stocks and typically pay high dividends. They include some of the least risky stocks and have consistent, stable growth. Examples include IBM and Universal Corp (IBM and UVV).

International Stocks

International stocks describe any stock that is issued outside of your home country. For example, any companies founded and based in Europe are considered international stocks to traders in the US. International stocks may also be called Foreign Stocks. Popular international stocks for US-based traders are Alibaba (BABA) and JD.com Inc. (JD).

Market Cap

Another common method of classification is through the total value of a company's shares, also referred to as the Market Cap. A market cap is found by multiplying the share price by the total number of shares. For example, a company with a $10 share price and 1 million shares has a market cap of $10 million. Most companies fall under the three main categories of small, mid or large cap, however, all six market cap classifications are listed below. Generally, the larger the market cap, the less risky a stock is.

- Nano-Cap - $50 Million and below

- Micro-Cap - $50 Million to $300 Million

- Small-Cap - Between $300 Million and $2 Billion

- Mid-Cap - Between $2 Billion and $10 Billion

- Large-Cap - Between $10 Billion and $200 Billion

- Mega-Caps - $200 Billion or more

Sectors

A third grouping of stocks is through the sectors in which they operate. Think of sectors as different parts of the economy. For example, healthcare is a sector that includes (among other sub-sectors) hospitals and drug companies. Different sectors have different benefits and downsides and move in similar directions. For example, some sectors are better to invest in during economic downturns and others during economic prosperity. It's important not only to know the different sectors but also to diversify your portfolio across multiple sectors. This way you can capture upside across multiple industries during different economic times and make your portfolio resistant to a large loss should a single sector decline. The stock market has 11 sectors, and all will be elaborated upon below.

Financials

Financial stocks include those of investment funds, banks, real estate firms, insurance companies, consumer finance companies, mortgage brokers and real estate trusts. While those all may sound intimidating, financial stocks all basically revolve around money, whether it's keeping your money or investing your money. Financial stocks often rise as interest rates rise because they make money from the mortgages and loans that they control, all of which benefit from increased interest rates. Companies in this sector include Bank Of America Corp (BAC), Morgan Stanley (MS) and Citigroup Inc. (C).

Energy

Energy stocks include power firms, refineries, oil and gas exploration companies, and production companies. Energy stocks will likely increase in value when the price of oil, natural gases, and other commodities rise. Companies in this sector include Exxon Mobile (XOM) and Chevron Corporation (CVX).

Utilities

The utility sector consists of water, electric, and gas companies. They are the companies that give you running water and electricity. The utility sector is known for earning stable and recurring income from its customers. Because of this, utility stock prices won't change much as the market goes up or down and are likely to pay high and consistent dividends. Companies include National Grid (NGG) and Dominion Resources (D).

Technology

Technology stocks consist of software developers, information technology firms and electronics manufacturers. These are the companies that research, produce, and sell the technology we buy. Technology stocks generally depend on the overall health of the market and the economy and tend to move with the market. Companies in this sector include Apple (AAPL), Microsoft (MSFT) and Amazon (AMZN).

Consumer Staples

Consumer staples companies produce food and beverages, as well as many other necessities. Consumer staples companies are resistant to economic downturns because even in times of financial struggle, people still need the necessities that these companies provide. Companies include Procter & Gamble (PG) and B & G Foods (BGS).

Consumer Discretionary

The consumer discretionary sector includes retail companies, media companies, and consumer service providers. Consumer discretionary companies are where consumers go shopping. The sector generally moves with the economy. Companies in this sector include McDonald's (MCD), Target (TGT) and Walmart (WMT).

Healthcare

Healthcare companies consist of hospital management firms, medical device marketers, biotechnology companies and many others. Some aspects of this sector are safer investments since people need healthcare no matter their financial situation, but many healthcare stocks, especially biotech's, are considered riskier because they are small and are often focused around one "make it or break it" product. Companies in this sector include Johnson & Johnson (JNJ), Kaiser Inc. (KGHI) and Biogen (BIIB).

Real Estate

The real estate sector consists of companies that invest in or manage all types of real estate. These companies make most of their money from rental income and capital appreciation from their holdings, and due to this, the sector and its stocks generally move with interest rates. Companies in the real estate sector include Host Hotels & Resorts Inc. (HST) and CBRE Group (CBRE).

Industrials

Industrial companies consist of aerospace, machinery, defense, construction, manufacturing, and fabrication companies. Industrial companies grow and fall alongside a demand for their products. Popular industrial stocks include Honeywell (HON), Ametek (AME) and Xylem (XYL).

Telecom

Telecom companies include cable companies, internet service and wireless providers, satellite companies and more. Since most people pay recurring payments for their internet and other services and aren't apt to change, the industry is usually consistent in earnings and growth. Just know that rapid change can come out of nowhere, as it did with PG&E Inc. (PCG), a gas and electricity provider that went from healthy to bankrupt after being sued billions for damages related to California wildfires. Verizon (VZ), AT&T (T) and Sprint Corporation (S) are some of the largest companies in the sector.

Materials

Material stocks consist of refining, chemical, forestry, and mining companies, along with any other developer of raw materials. These companies generally rise and fall with the economy because of their precarious position at the bottom of the supply chain. Material companies include Ecolab Inc. (ECL) and DuPont de Nemours Inc. (DD).

Types of Investments

→ learn

There are many types of investments that go beyond the basic buying and selling of a stock. This section will include the most popular methods, of which there are many, however, understand that buying and selling of stocks, mutual funds, and index funds are all you need to be doing for at least the first year of investing. Only pursue other methods once you're comfortable with the basics.

Stocks

Stocks are the most basic form of investing in the stock market. When you buy a stock, you buy a very small piece of that company. For example, if Amazon has 100 million shares of its company available and you buy one share, you now own 0.000000001% of Amazon. For that share to increase in value people must be willing to pay more for the stock than what you paid for it. For example, if you bought that 1 share of Amazon at $100 and the stock went to $150, you could sell it and make $50 in profit. Some stocks may also offer dividends. Dividends are when companies pay you for owning shares of their stock. For example, if I bought one share of Johnson & Johnson at $140, they might pay me 50 cents every quarter, or $2.00 a year for owning that share. Dividends are a safe way to make money that many people use to create a stable income source for themselves.

Mutual Funds

Mutual funds and index funds (preferably index funds due to lower fees) are the only other option that I suggest investing in immediately after you open an account because of their stability and simplicity. Mutual funds allow you to invest in a diverse group of stocks in a portfolio that's managed by a professional fund manager. Imagine it like this: let's say you want to buy Apple, Amazon and Microsoft stock. Each of the stocks trade at $100, but you only have $50 dollars to invest. You could then look for a mutual fund in which the fund manager finds 6 people just like you. Combined, those 6 people have the $300 needed to invest in all 3 companies. You each invest your $50, and then you own a little bit (less than one share) of each of the companies. This is how mutual funds operate, although most are on a much larger scale. For example, a mutual fund might include the top 500 companies on the market. Think of it as being able to invest in many stocks with significantly less capital than it would otherwise take. Mutual funds are considered safe investments because of their low volatility and steady growth.

Index Funds

An index fund is a mutual fund; with the only difference being index funds are not actively managed. Two of the most popular funds in the US are the Fidelity ZERO Large Cap Index and Schwab's S&P 500 index funds. Index funds are historically good investments and due to their popularity, index funds hold more than $4 trillion in assets and comprise 14% of the American stock market.

REIT

A REIT, meaning Real Estate Investment Trust, is a company that operates, owns, or finances income-producing (either residential or commercial) real estate. A REIT will own a portfolio of many properties, not just one, and hundreds of REITS are listed on the market. As an investment, REITs are historically extremely volatile.

Shorting

Short selling, known as shorting a stock, is the alternative to buying stock. When you buy stocks, you're betting that the company's stock price will go up. When you short a stock, you're betting that the stock will go down. Shorting is a risky investment due to the potentially large losses it may incur, but once you're experienced enough and have some spare money it's great to try it out and learn.

Options

Many people find options intimidating, but if the time is taken to learn about them, they're a great way to lessen the risk of investments. In fact, you use options all the time in your day-to-day life. Think of an option as getting a coupon to buy a pizza for $10 at your favorite restaurant. The coupon will expire in 6 months. Let's say you go into the pizza restaurant and the pizza is being sold for $12. You might want to then use your coupon, but if the pizza restaurant is now selling pizzas for $8 apiece, you might want to hold on to the coupon until the price goes higher and you can get a discount. That's exactly what real options do. Options give you the right to buy or sell a stock at a given price within a certain time period. For example, you might buy an option for 100 shares of Apple at $100. If the stock climbs to $150, you might execute the order and buy those 100 shares for $100. Once you buy, you can immediately sell the shares you bought at $100 for $150 and make $50 per share. There are two types of options: Call options and Put options. Call options give you the right to buy a stock at a given price, while Put options give you the right to sell a stock at a given price. For example, if you buy a Put option for 100 shares of Apple at $200 and the stock goes down to $150, you're allowed to sell those shares at $200 even though the stock is only at $150. Options get much more complicated than this and E*TRADE has tutorial videos that delve much deeper into the topic. Visit the resources section in Part VI for links to E*TRADE's content.

How to Understand the Fundamentals

Understanding a few of the key metrics and numbers of what form the fundamentals of a company can greatly increase your chances of making good investments. You can find the following information for a stock on all major online investment websites, typically on the summary page. To find this information for free, visit finance.yahoo.com. In the following section, we'll focus on the ten most important fundamental metrics to help you understand a company.

The Big Ten — learn all

1. Open
2. 52-Week Range
3. Average Volume
4. EPS
5. P/E
6. Next Earnings Date
7. Market Cap
8. Shares Outstanding
9. Beta
10. Dividend Yield

Open

The open price of a stock is the price that the stock opened at for a day. For example, Apple might be trading at $350, but the open price could be $345. The open price can help to determine the volatility of a stock and the movement of the market without looking at a chart.

52-Week Range

This metric displays the range in which a stock has traded at over the last year. For example, during the last year, if a stock hit a low of $4.00 in September and hit a high of $6.00 in November, the 52-week range would be $4.00 - $6.00. The 52-week range of a stock can help determine the amount of growth the stock has had and whether it's the right time to buy. A stock that's trading at $55.00 and has a 52-week range of $20 to $60 might not be a great investment because the stock has already nearly tripled in the year. Likewise, buying a stock that's halved in value and is trading near the low end of its 52-week range might be a bad investment decision. Overall, use this tool to make sure the stock you want to invest in has room to grow while not being in the dumps.

Average Volume

The volume of a stock, as you may remember, is the number of times a stock has been traded. The average volume simply displays the average amount of times a stock had been traded within a specified length of time, typically 10 days.

EPS

EPS, or earnings per share, calculates a company's profit divided by the number of total shares a company offers for its stocks. The resulting ratio acts as an indicator of the company's profitability. The higher the EPS the better, however, don't exclude a company simply based on its EPS because the EPS doesn't consider the health and situation of a company, only it's stock.

P/E Ratio

P/E stands for price-to-earnings. A P/E ratio compares a stock's share price against the amount of money the company makes per share. For example, let's use Tesla (TSLA). Let's say TSLA is trading at $800 and making $80 per share. 800 (the price) ÷ 80 (the earnings per share, or EPS) = 10. Therefore, Tesla would have a P/E ratio of 10. While P/E ratios vary per industry and sector, a very high P/E ratio or a very low P/E ratio generally isn't good. However, keep in mind that small startups, which may potentially have huge growth potential but aren't making money, typically have low P/E ratios and therefore are exceptions to the rule. Don't judge a stock solely based on its P/E ratio; just keep it in mind as a factor to consider.

Next Earnings Date

Next earnings date, or earnings date, refers to the next date a company reports quarterly earnings. Refer to the basic terms section for information on quarters and earnings.

Market Cap

The market cap (refer to the terms section for a definition) determines the size of a company. Generally, the smaller a company is, the riskier the investment is because the company has a greater chance of going out of business.

Shares Outstanding

When a company is first listed on the market, that company issues a total number of shares of its stock for investors to own and trade. That number, the total amount of shares in a company, is called the shares outstanding. Companies can add or buy back shares to increase or decrease the total number of shares on the market.

Beta

The beta of a stock represents that stock's volatility in relation to the market. Any number below 1 means that a given stock is less volatile than the market, while anything over 1 means that a given stock is more volatile than the overall market. The beta number is a good indication of the volatility and therefore (typically, but not always) the risk of a stock.

Dividend Yield

As defined in the terms section, a dividend yield represents the percentage of a stock price that you earn in dividends each year. Generally, stocks that have stable dividends are safer than stocks without dividends. A dividend basically means a company is paying you to own their stock and any company that can afford to pay a dividend, even a small one, is less likely to go out of business or crash. The downside is that large companies with dividends are likely to be slow growers and have less potential upside than small companies. The dividend norm for large companies is 1% to 3%.

This concludes the big ten fundamental metrics of a company. These key metrics lay the groundwork to develop a deep knowledge of a company and its stock.

Understanding Earnings

As a reminder, earnings reports are issued quarterly by a company to provide insight into performance. Earnings, both good and bad, can have a huge impact on a stock price, and understanding the basics of a quarterly earnings report is invaluable in choosing good investments. Companies are legally required to submit a quarterly report, of which the following contain the most useful information for investors. The following documents are collectively part of a company's financial statements.

- Income Statement
- Balance Sheet
- Cash Flow Statement
- Q&A and Predictions

Income Statement

An income statement shows a company's revenues, expenses, and profit. Each category (revenues, expenses, and profits) is broken down into subsections. Revenue displays the total revenue as well as the cost of goods sold (COGS) and the gross profit. All the numbers on an income statement, as well as on all of the documents in this section, are typically in millions, not thousands. The expenses section should show all expenses, from marketing to salaries and insurance. Finally, the taxes and then profits will be displayed. Income sheets are a great quick way to assess a company's financial situation.

Balance Sheet

Balance sheets reveal the assets, liabilities, and the owner's equity of a company. The most important information lies in the assets and liabilities sections. The assets section breaks down all of the assets a company owns. One large asset type is called current assets. Current assets, comprising of cash and short-term investments (also known as cash and cash equivalents), inventory, and accounts receivables are any assets that can easily be sold or converted into cash. Another asset type is called long-term assets, or not-current assets. Long-term assets can include machinery, equipment, land, and patents; all assets that are difficult to liquidate quickly. Subtract the current assets from the total assets to find the long-term assets.

That covers assets; next up on a balance sheet is liabilities (or debt that is owed). Look for total current liabilities (which are liabilities that must be paid within one year) and long-term debt (sometimes known as long-term liabilities). Long-term debt covers any liabilities that must be paid in full at least one year or more out from the date of the report. Total liabilities will combine all the current and long-term liabilities into one number. Make sure to note whether a company has been paying down liabilities and adding to its assets within the last couple of years of a report. Collectively, those numbers help you understand and use the important metrics on a balance sheet.

Cash Flow Statement

A cash flow statement comprises the amount of cash and cash equivalents (cash equivalents are assets that are easy to liquidate) moving through a company. A cash flow statement consists of three parts: Cash from operating, cash from investing and cash from financing. Cash from operating is any cash made from the business's products or services. Cash from investing comprises cash flow from the assets and investments of a company. Cash from financing covers money from investors and banks, as well as dividends and stock repurchases. Overall, use the cash flow statement to determine whether a company is gaining or losing cash as well as whether a company is raising money through debt or through revenue.

As a side note, cash flow is a very important financial lesson for any person looking to be financially free later in life. To read more about cash flow and how it impacts your life as well as the type of investments you should make outside of the stock market, make sure to read the Robert Kiyosaki books in the resources section.

Q&A and Predictions

Companies will usually make predictions for the upcoming quarter or year during an earnings report. These predictions are likely to impact a stock price based on whether the company predicts it will perform well. As well as predictions, earnings will usually contain a Q&A section where analysts can ask questions. These Q&A sections often show important information about the company that otherwise wouldn't be revealed. Overall, use these two categories as a source of further information about the stock's future potential.

How Do I Find This Information?

Earning calls, as well as financial documents, are publicly available and not difficult to gain access to. To view financials as well as financial statements for free, use any of the following sites:

- **US Securities and Exchange Commission**
    - https://www.sec.gov/edgar.shtml
- **Yahoo! Finance**
    - finance.yahoo.com
- **Google Finance**
    - finance.google.com

As mentioned above, company's earnings calls are usually publicly available. Many companies offer a phone number that can be accessed to listen live as they deliver their quarterly reports. Listening to a quarterly report live is a great experience and is definitely something you should try. Just choose your favorite company and visit their website. All the information you need should be under a tab called "Investors" or something of the like. In fact, many companies also display their financial statements on their website along with press releases and news.

By now, you should understand the most important numbers released in a quarterly report. To delve further into the world of earnings, visit the resources section, and you have now completed Part III: Stock Market Literacy. There's truly an entire world of stock market investing filled with more than could be fit into this book, but the bases should be covered. In fact, you may have heard some words or terms that weren't covered. If you have any, take a moment to remember them and write them down:

_____   _____

_____   _____

_____   _____

_____   _____

At this point, you should be able to understand all the basic metrics and terms that are commonly used. This information will lay the groundwork for picking good stocks. However, the second part of choosing good investments is in developing a strategy that fits your goals and lifestyle.

Part IV: Stock Market Strategy for Teenagers

Developing a core strategy and the discipline to stick to it is instrumental in investing. Different strategies fit different people and finding your perfect strategy is the next step in the process to becoming a successful investor. Picking a strategy starts with the person. For example, a middle-aged person with a family to provide for will be more inclined to invest in safe dividend-paying stocks. However, a young and ambitious investor might be interested in a riskier portfolio that may potentially have more upside.

Now, I want you to take a minute and ask yourself what your goal is in investing; Are you just interested in learning about the stock market? Are you looking for some extra cash? Do you want to become a multi-millionaire through stocks? Once you have your answer, think about what type of investing will serve you the best. Here are several factors to keep in mind as well as the recommended strategy for investing as a teenager.

As a rule for investing young, think long term. The great (and profitable) thing about investing at an early age is that your money has decades to grow. You don't need to take huge risks because (remember compound interest) your money will exponentially increase over time. If you can make

8% profit per year (historically low for the market), each $100 you invest will be worth just under $5,000 in 50 years. If you invest well and make 10% per year, that $100 invested will become $11,739 in 50 years. You can check it out for yourself on a compound interest calculator. My favorite compound interest calculator is Moneychimp's calculator. You can check it out at this link:

http://www.moneychimp.com/calculator/compound_interest_calculator.htm

Unfortunately, 50 years is a long time. However, you need to understand that being patient and being smart can provide financial security that few are fortunate enough to have. It's not worth risking huge chunks of your portfolio on risky investments to make an extra 10%, while over time your money can 50x, 80x or even 100x itself.

Based on this thinking, I recommend that teenagers play the long game if they're truly interested in stocks and having financial freedom later in life. A long-term stock market strategy will typically include large-cap, value and dividend paying stocks, as well as some growth stocks and index or mutual funds. Growth stocks will likely go through periods of high growth and buying and selling of those stocks should be performed accordingly. While many value stocks are slow growers and don't need much attention, putting some money into growth stocks should allow you to engage more in the market as well as make some extra money.

You don't by any means have to follow this strategy, and if you would rather do something else with your profits than reinvesting, such as funding your lifestyle, that's fine, just understand what you're sacrificing. If it's worth it to you, then go ahead and do it. Additionally, if a long-term strategy doesn't suit your style, just try something different. A long-term, value/growth stock and index/mutual fund investing strategy is recommended because it has historically led to the highest return and is a good fit for most people, but an emphasis should be placed on "most."

I personally love investing in small and upcoming stocks. I've seen stocks double or triple (check out the real-life examples in Part V) but also halve. To stay active in investing and keep it fun, I incorporate investing in those up-and-coming companies into my strategy. Although trading with a long-term mindset is recommended for teens, understand that due to your age, putting money in some risky investments is completely fine. However, make sure to have rules. I only invest 25% of the money (per trade) that I otherwise would into risky stocks (for example, $1000 put in a relatively safe stock and $250 in an up-and-coming stock) and if I'm down 10% I immediately sell, no matter the upside. While this may have cost me some serious gains, it's saved my money from equally serious losses. These rules let my money grow safely while having fun and taking extra profit on the side.

Now that you have developed an overall strategy and you understand the technical aspects of stocks, it's time to dive into picking good investments that are tailored to your overall stock market strategy. For example, someone with a long-term orientation who wants to "invest and forget" will place a focus on index funds, mutual funds, and slow growing blue-chip stocks. To find these companies, I generally recommend two routes that can be used simultaneously. First, as elaborated upon in the book, *One Up On Wall Street* by Peter Lynch, look around you. Spotting trends and products before they become hot stocks is a great method as long as potential investments are thoroughly researched. However, many great companies won't ever reach your location, so the second method to find great companies is through a stock screener. If you've already signed up for an online trading platform, chances are you already have access to one. If not, several free alternatives are available. Here are some of the best:

- o https://finance.yahoo.com/screener
- o https://www.tradingview.com/screener

Stock screeners basically allow you to use filters to sort through the thousands of stocks out there and find stocks that fit into your investment strategy. Let's walk through the stock screener process by identifying some of the filters I might set if I was looking for a small, volatile company with potentially good upwards movement to invest in:

Market Cap: Micro Cap and Small Cap

Price: Greater than $1, less than $50 (try to stay away from stocks under $1)

Sector: All

Industry: All

Price Change: Greater than 10% during the last 30 days (either up or down: indicates volatility)

Price Performance versus the S&P: 20% - 40% during the last 52 weeks (this results in stocks that are beating the market)

P/E ratio: Above Industry Average

Within: 10% of its 52-week high (this means a stock is near its high for the year and hasn't dropped)

Revenue Growth Annual: 25% - 50% and >50%

EPS Growth: Positive Change

If I plug those exact filters into a stock screener (I use E*TRADE's), these 15 companies meet the criteria:

      ATAX - America First Multifamily Investors LP
      ACLS - Axcelis Technologies Inc.
      DHT - DHT Holdings Inc
      EARN - Ellington residential Mortgage REIT
      EBMS - First Bancshares Inc
      FCPT - Four Corners Property Trust Inc
      GMRE - Global Medical REIT Inc
      HTHT - Huazhue Group Ltd (ADR)
      KRNT - Kornit Digital Ltd

KLIC - Kulicke and Soffa Industries Inc.

OFG- OFG Bancorp

RWT - Redwood Trust, Inc.

SASR - Sandy Spring Bancorp Inc.

TPVG – Triplepoint Venture Growth BDC Corp

VCTR – Victory Capital Holdings Inc

Out of the 15 stocks that met my criteria, I can now examine the sectors. I'm not looking to invest in REITs (because interest rates may be down), so I can remove those from the list. I'm not looking to invest in Oil & Gas (because the price of oil may be down), so I can remove DHT holdings Inc. Banking may not be hot, so Sandy Spring Bancorp Inc., OFG Bancorp, America First Multifamily Investors LP, and First Bancshares Inc. are out. TPVG and VCTR, investment companies, are also out. The results are the following stocks:

Kornit Digital Ltd. (KRNT)

Kulicke and Soffa Industries Inc. (KLIC)

Huazhu Group Ltd. (HTHT)

Axcelis Technologies Inc. (ACLS)

As you can see, a stock screener allowed me to go from thousands of potential companies down to 4 that perfectly match my criteria. Stock screeners are a great way to find great investments, and the filters used were just the basics. Dozens of other criteria and filters can be applied, so take some time to play around and see what you come up with.

Part IV: Stock Market Strategy for Teenagers

What to do When Everything's Going Down

Sadly, not everything goes up all the time. If a correction or crash happens, the entire market may be moving downward. Knowing what to do during these times can not only save you money, but also make you money.

First, understand that bear markets and corrections are historically short-term. Basically, during most bear markets throughout history, you could completely ignore a crash and your portfolio would be recovered within 5 years. Therefore, the best bet to make money while stocks are going down is to hold your important investments, raise some cash and buy the best deals as close to the market's low as you can.

To elaborate, sell stocks that will recover the slowest or fall the farthest; then buy stocks near their low that have fallen the farthest and are likely to recover the quickest. For example, during the 2020 crash, I heavily bought into Tesla (TSLA) around its $350 low and up to $550 because I'm certain Tesla's stock will be back to it's near $1000 high within 5 years of the crash. On the other hand, I'll sell a stock like Johnson & Johnson (JNJ), which is generally recession-proof and won't move much. This way, I can use a market downturn to my advantage and maybe even turn a profit. This method bets on the market recovering relatively quickly, while an economic depression would be a different story. Also know it's fine to hold stocks that won't move much like J&J if you have enough cash to take advantage of any opportunities.

To identify the stocks that will rebound the highest you must first identify the stocks that have lost the most value simply because the market went down; not because of an actual business issue related to the cause of the crash or correction. For example, Tesla lost more than 60% of its value, falling from around $950 to a low of $350 during 2020. At the same time, Carnival (CCL), a cruise tour operator, fell from a high of roughly $50 to just under $10, resulting in an 80% reduction in share value. While Carnival may seem like a better deal as opposed to Tesla, Carnival is affected much more by the core cause of the crash than Tesla is. As a result, it may be better to purchase Tesla because Tesla is likely to recover quicker.

The question then is: When to buy? The most important advice to remember is that it's okay not to perfectly time the bottom of a crash. It's better to buy Tesla at $500 and ride it to $900 than to attempt but fail to buy it at $300 and miss out on the gain. Buying 5% - 10% off a market's low will still result in greater gains within a couple of years than not purchasing at all. In my experience, it's somewhat easy to tell when the worst of a crash is over, such as after a 30% drop in one week occurs. Even if the market might lose another 10% after it's 30% drop, buying would still fall within the recommended 5% - 10% buy-in off a low during a crash or correction. To sum it up, just keep calm and don't be emotional. The advice above historically would allow for the most profit during a crash or correction, but every situation is different, so you may need to make your own decisions based on your unique circumstances. Finally, remember this: nothing, neither a bull market nor a bear market, lasts forever.

Before moving on, take a minute to summarize the overall trading style and strategy that you think will work best for you, your situation, and your personality.

80% into safe slow growth / dividend investments

20% higher risk potenial

As well as developing an overall strategy for your money, it's important to understand some fundamental rules, concepts, and strategies that dictate when to buy and when to sell stocks, starting with the rule of opposites.

The Rule of Opposites

The rule of opposites is the idea that a smart investor will (in most situations) do the opposite of the market. This applies only to money that is invested in short-term holdings, which are stocks that are bought with the intent to sell within one year. Basically, the rule of opposites dictates that if the market is moving up, an investor will gradually sell. If the market is going down, an investor will slowly buy. Remember, markets that are moving up will likely experience a correction (a short-term dip) within 5 years. This follows a simple logic: If everyone is making money, it can't last. This was proven in 2008 by the crash of the housing market and the stock market with it. The economy can't indefinitely make money for all parties involved and therefore corrections and crashes are necessary. However, historically speaking, US stock markets have had extremely long bull markets, with the most recent one lasting 11 years. Based on this, a smart investor won't sell all, or even most of their holdings during a great market. Money invested in dividend stocks and stocks bought for the long-term shouldn't be sold. Stocks rising just because the market is rising, and risky investments are great investments to slowly sell as a market goes up. For example, for each 10% the market moves up, you might sell 5% of your holdings and keep them in cash. As an alternative, you might try some day trading with some of the money otherwise held in cash.

As mentioned, the market won't always go up. Corrections are liable to happen. However, dips in the market shouldn't be seen as bad. Instead, they should be viewed as opportunities to buy. Within the last decade, 32 bear markets have occurred in the US market. They occur on average every 3 - 4 years and last, on average, just over 1 year. Remember, to a long-term investor, 1 year is just a blip. Most markets rebound quickly from dips and rise to even greater heights. Based on this, a smart investor will buy as the market goes down. For example, for each 5% the market goes down; invest 10% of your portfolio (or 10% of your cash). Since corrections reduce, on average, 13% of a market's value, a one-year recession that rebounds over a two-year span can result in 20% of a portfolio making 20% greater profits.

Understanding the Economy

It's important to understand good stocks and bad stocks to buy during a specific economic period. During economic downturns, stocks that sell necessities like toilet paper, clothes, medical supplies (such as Band-Aids) and food are the best investments. Stocks like these will often go up during a correction. Examples are Johnson & Johnson (JNJ), a company that focuses on medical devices and pharmaceuticals, Ross Stores (ROST), a discount clothes retailer, and Walmart (WMT), a discount store chain.

During times of war, invest in companies like Lockheed Martin (LMT), General Dynamics (GD) and Northrop Grumman (NOC). All these companies produce defense equipment and weapons. During a war, governments spend billions on contracts with companies like these.

During a thriving economy, move some money into stocks with high growth potential. A good economy can act as a safety net and propel stocks that otherwise wouldn't perform as well.

So, look at the economy around you. Do some research and figure out what stocks are set to most profit from your country's situation. You may even want to consider investing in international stocks if you've done your research and determined that an international company is an opportunity, perhaps based on its country's economic situation. To sum it up, pay attention to your surroundings and act accordingly.

Cutting Losses

A foolproof method to prevent losing money is to have rules of when to sell a stock if money is being lost. For example, I personally have a 10% rule. Every time I buy a stock, I will issue an indefinite sell order 10% below the price I entered at. If the stock tanks, I cut my losses at 10%. Unfortunately, this trick can sometimes backfire. Stocks may fall 10% and then rebound to new highs. However, I find that the 10% rule prevents more losses than the gains it protects. If you believe in a stock and you know it's volatile, set a sell order 20% below, or 30%. Rules like this are simply good precautions to have in place.

Don't Be Emotional

While this may not exactly be a strategy, it's a very important rule to follow. Investing because of short-term emotion is nearly always faulty. Don't trade based on one article, one day, or one drop. If an emotional buyer sees their favorite stock drop 10%, they might freak out and sell. However, a smart and disciplined investor will do the research, discover that the 10% dip shouldn't impact future performance, and buy more shares. Differences like that add up over time. If you really can't stand volatility in a stock and know you're an emotional investor, alter your overall investing strategy. Invest in stocks that are less volatile and resistant to downturns. Diversify your portfolio to reduce the risk of a downturn in one segment affecting a large portion of your portfolio and always keep some cash on hand to ease worries. Just remember, try not to trade emotionally as much as possible.

Diversify

As mentioned, specific segments, industries, or stocks are sometimes subject to downturns even if the entire market isn't. Based on this, it's important to diversify your portfolio to reduce the risk of one specific event causing a massive loss. For example, a portfolio invested only in gas station companies could take massive hits as electric cars become more and more popular. Make sure to research the cycle of sectors and diversify based on that information. <u>Invest in many different sectors</u>, in companies of different size, and in companies with different levels of risk. Diversifying your portfolio lessens risk across the board and results a much more stable portfolio.

Prices Don't Matter

One last lesson to remember and practice is that prices don't matter. Too often, stocks are purchased, or not purchased, based on its share price. However, you need to understand that a $10 stock and a $1000 stock aren't inherently better or worse than one another solely based on price. If equal amounts of money are put in, the same return will be generated. For example, let's say 100 shares of a $10 stock are bought along with 1 share of a $1000 stock. The $1000 stock might move up $100, while the $10 stock might move up $1. Despite the differences in share price, the value of the 100 shares and the 1 share would then both be $1100. This means that the price doesn't matter, only the amount of money invested matters. In fact, the price doesn't signify anything about a stock by itself and prices are often changed due to stock splits. If you can't afford an expensive stock, that's fine, but for share prices that you can afford, remember that the price doesn't signify anything. (Fun Fact: One of Berkshire Hathaway's stocks, listed as BRK.A, is currently trading in the hundreds of thousands.)

Trade What You Know

A great rule of thumb to make good investments is to trade what you know and what is around you. For a teen, this might be the newest trend at school. Spotting trends before they reach their climax and investing in companies that would capitalize on the trend can result in some great picks. Be attentive to new products and ideas around you all the time, such as at a job, at home, a mall, or online. Use your specific skills and knowledge to identify potential investments. If you love gaming and you've heard a new game will change the gaming landscape, find the company that created that game. Trading what you know and catching trends before they hit their stride can yield big gains. As previously mentioned, this concept is further exemplified in Peter Lynch's book *One Up On Wall Street*.

Buy Damaged Stocks, Not Damaged Companies

The difference between a damaged stock and a damaged company (credit to *The Street*) is the difference between making and losing money and it's instrumental to understand the difference. Damaged companies are companies that have suffered a long-term hit to their revenue, reputation, or products, and will take years to recover. Damaged stocks are stocks that fell because of an event causing a short-term impact or even due to something completely unrelated to the company. For example, Chipotle once unknowingly spread a virus through their food. This caused their stock to take a massive hit as well as destroying their reputation and sales. At that time, Chipotle would be a damaged company and not a good investment. However, imagine that a celebrity ordered Chipotle and had an allergic reaction. That celebrity proceeded to attack the company on social media, resulting in a 10% decrease in the stock price. In this situation, since the allergic reaction doesn't signify any problems with the company, Chipotle would be a damaged stock and therefore a good potential investment. Use this rule of thumb to determine whether issues affecting a company render it a potential investment.

No Woulda, Shoulda, Coulda

This rule, with credit again going to Jim Cramer and *The Street*, provides a tip on how to stay sane in the market. As a rule, stay away from ever saying woulda, shoulda, or coulda. Since so many stocks trade on the market, you'll always hear about amazing market movers and stocks that went up 30% in a day or 500% in a year. You might sell a stock that proceeded to go up 100% in the next month. You might buy a stock that goes down 50% the week after you buy it. Whatever happens, never say "I shoulda sold it..." or "If only I held on..." Doing those things leads to a destructive and self-sabotaging mindset. Understand that deals are everywhere, and mistakes will be made. Just go along for the ride and don't look back.

Now, write two or three of your favorite ideas and rules from the list above that made the most impact on you so that you never forget them and can easily revisit them:

Have a safety net, limit

Do the proper research

Price doesn't reflect potential

Trade what I understand

Part V: In Practice

The first section of Part 5 contains both successful and unsuccessful real-life examples of stock market trades that I have made as a teenager. Throughout this section, make sure to note both what worked and what didn't. All charts are on a 1-year time span unless otherwise noted.

Real-Life Examples

Apple (AAPL)

Apple, the technology company we all know and love, was entering some of its best years in 2018. I chose this company to invest in based on several factors. First, the company had strong fundamentals, strong earnings, and strong analyst predictions. I also noticed that products like the AirPods were hitting their stride in the school I went to. I felt the company was undervalued and bought in at $160. Around a year later, I began to sell my position at $280 and later $360. I still hold half of the original investment at the time of this publication. This stock was a winner for me because careful research showed an undervalued company and is a reminder that large companies, even trillion-dollar companies, can still have huge growth in a short time. 1 year update (2021): Apple conducted a 4-1 stock split and I maintain a 200% gain.

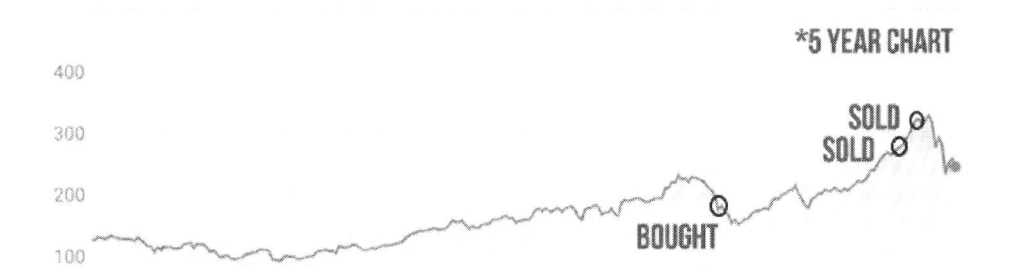

notice trend

*5 YEAR CHART

SOLD
SOLD

BOUGHT

Fortress Biotech (FBIO)

Fortress Biotech is a small biotechnology company that identifies and develops biotechnology and pharmaceutical products. At the time I purchased it, Fortress Biotech had a pipeline (meaning products in development) filled with very promising drugs. I recognized the potential and bought in at $1.80 and $1.90. While I don't normally invest in stocks this cheap, FBIO was growing steadily and seemed to be in a strong position, unlike many of its penny stock peers. Less than three months after purchasing, I sold my shares at $2.45, representing a more than 30% gain. Furthermore, the only reason I sold my position was in preparation for the coronavirus-caused market crash of 2020. Soon after, the volatile stock was hit hard and fell to $1.10. However, keep in mind the rule: Buy damaged stocks, not damaged companies. FBIO lost more than 50% due to a crash whose core causes had no impact on their long-term business. Therefore, I purchased an even larger position than I originally owned at $1.10. As of this writing, FBIO is closing is on $4.00, which is more than a 385% gain over the original point of entry. As of this second update, I've since sold my entire position at the 400% gain.

Tandem Diabetes Care (TNDM)

Tandem, a small healthcare company focused on developing diabetes treatments, underwent a massive surge throughout 2018 and 2019. The stock went from 50 cents to nearly $50, a 1000% jump, in just over a year. I liked the company and I wanted to get in on the hype surrounding it, so I established a position at $45. Two months later, it had done nothing but fall and I sold my entire position at $33. Tandem became my worst loss to date. Both the buy and the sell were done emotionally and without research, something that always sets trades up to fail. Following my sale, the company climbed to $70 and passed $80 soon after. Remember, intelligent trading is done without emotion and instead with careful research.

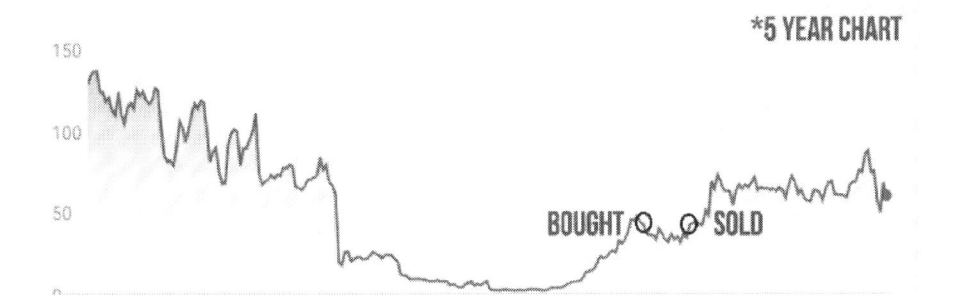

Set to fail / up

*5 YEAR CHART

Netflix (NFLX)

Netflix, the streaming media and content production company that changed the face of the entertainment industry, was enjoying years of dominance and free reign in the streaming business during the early 2010s. At the time, I'd worked hard and was ready for my first multi-thousand dollar trade. Using concepts exemplified in *One Up On Wall Street*, I only had to look around me to identify a potential investment. I didn't have to look far to see that Netflix was becoming a household staple and that it was releasing hit after hit, including the recently released *Stranger Things*. My family began to use the platform to watch movies and research backed up my view of Netflix as a company with huge potential and strong fundamentals. Based on this, I bought in at $180 and again at $190. I began to trade out of my position a year and a half later, respectively at $323 and $363. This rich reward in such a short time is a result of trading what I knew. Using what's around you, whether it's a new trending product or a fast-food chain everyone's talking about, is a great way to find potentially lucrative investments.

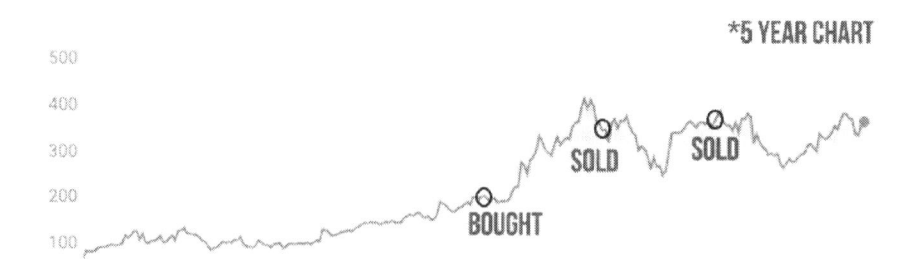

*5 YEAR CHART

Proofpoint (PFPT)

Proofpoint was an example of a lazy trade, made based on news and not research. At the time I bought it, I'd heard a good piece of news about it on an investment show and the look of the company appealed to me. With no research and no strategy, I bought it at $118. I was given what I deserved, and although I managed to sell before the collapse to $80, I took a 20% loss (this was before my 10% stop loss rule) in just over a month on a stock I shouldn't have bought in the first place. Remember, always do your homework, and find multiple views before trading based on news. As a second lesson, holding onto an investment you're down on (in a bull market) will likely erase losses if held onto long enough. → don't rely on this fact

Take-Two Interactive (TTWO)

Take-Two Interactive is a video game company responsible for major hits including Grand Theft Auto, NBA 2k, WWE 2k, Civilization, Red Dead Redemption, Borderlands, and Bioshock. In February of 2020, Take-Two Interactive reported earnings that caused more than a 10% decrease in stock price. TTWO has a long track record of beating guidance and smashing expectations, so when the quarterly earnings only met expectations, instead of exceeding them, the stock dropped. The performance was in part due to a failed game launch and the news that NBA 2k wouldn't have a record year, two factors which wouldn't impact long-term potential. The leadership team at Take-Two Interactive took ownership of the issues and promised to improve. This is an example of a damaged stock instead of a damaged company. However, since almost immediately after buying into this stock the COVD-19 pandemic triggered a stock market crash and dragged the entire market down, this is also an example of how timing can make or break a trade whether that trade would otherwise have been successful. Since I wasn't yet up 10% on my investment, I normally would have sold, but in this case, I didn't sell due to the "buy damaged stocks, not damaged companies" rule. Based on this, I continue to hold the stock (2021 update: I've since sold at a 60% profit).

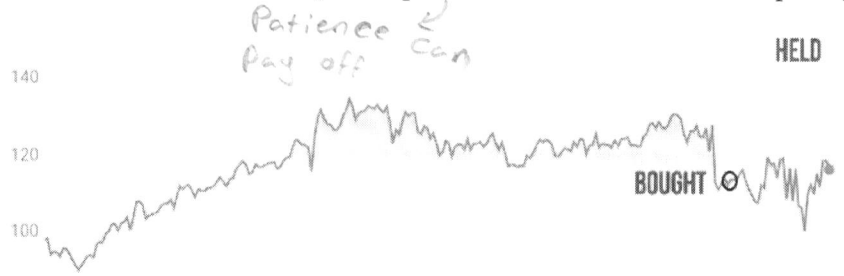

Patience & Pay off can

HELD

BOUGHT

2nd Edition Trading Update

This is an update from June of 2021, more than 1 year after this book was originally published. It's been a crazy year (covid!) and, at least in the market, an amazing one. Here are my biggest winners and biggest losers since the 1st edition:

Winners
- Tesla (TSLA): 500% gain
- CGE Energy (CGEI): 140% gain
- Planet 13 (PLNF): 106% gain
- Ford (F): 75% gain

Losers
- The Lion Electric Company (LEV): 43% loss
- Coinbase (COIN): 29% loss
- CytoDyn (CYDY): 19% loss

Takeaway:

Write down the most important lesson, or lessons, you learned from these real-life examples:

Research

look for trends - everyday life

Stick to rules

Have a tolerance & patience

From The Experts

As part of the real-life section, we will investigate the wisdom of the world's top investors. Remember, learning is the best thing you can do to ensure future success, especially in the stock market. Learning from the best will make you a smart and better investor. Take some time to look for patterns in the philosophies while reading.

Warren Buffet

[handwritten margin note: don't stop learning]

1. "The best investment you can make is an investment in yourself. The more you learn, the more you earn."

2. "Be fearful when others are greedy and greedy when others are fearful." *[handwritten: → take the risk others won't]*

3. "Our favorite holding period is forever.

Investing Philosophy: Warren Buffett, widely considered the most successful investor of all time, preaches investing in value and holding for long periods of time or until the stock price reflects the true value of a company. Buffet's company, Berkshire Hathaway, currently manages hundreds of billions of dollars and has averaged a 20% return since 1965.

Fun Fact: Warren Buffet described Benjamin Graham's book *The Intelligent Investor* as "by far the best book on investing ever written."

Benjamin Graham

1. "The intelligent investor is a realist who sells to optimists and buys from pessimists."

2. "Investing isn't about beating others at their game. It's about controlling yourself at your game."

3. "Successful investing is about managing risk, not avoiding it."

Investing Philosophy: Since Benjamin Graham mentored Warren Buffet, the pair has a very similar philosophy. Graham's trading philosophy is now called the Benjamin method and is based on value investing. In fact, Graham is credited as the godfather of value investing and popularized it during the early 1930s. During his professional trading career, Graham averaged a more than 20% return while the market averaged 12%.

Fun Fact: Benjamin Graham personally taught Warren Buffet while Buffet studied at Columbia University. Graham influenced Buffet so much that Warren Buffet's first son is named Howard Graham Buffet.

Seth Klarman

1. "The single greatest edge an investor can have is a long-term orientation."

2. "Investing is the orientation of economics and psychology."

3. "The stock market is the story of cycles and of the human behavior that is responsible for overreactions in both directions."

Investing Philosophy: Seth Klarman is a value investor who places a focus on risk, or the lack thereof. He places risk analysis at the forefront of his strategy and doesn't invest without complete certainty that a total loss won't occur. Currently, Klarman has a net worth of $1.5 billion.

Fun Fact: An out-of-print book written by Seth Klarman called *Margin Of Safety* was so coveted that used copies once sold for $2,500. Then, in 2018, it was made available on Amazon's Kindle store for $9.99.

Sir John Templeton

1. "The 4 most dangerous words in investing are "This time it's different." → market always changing

2. "Bull markets are born on pessimism, grow on skepticism, mature on optimism and die on euphoria."

3. "The time of maximum pessimism is the best time to buy, and the time of maximum optimism is the best time to sell." → buy ↓ / sell ↑

Investing Philosophy: John Templeton followed the simple investing strategy of "buy low, sell high." He reinvented value investing by taking it "to an extreme, picking nations, industries, and companies hitting rock-bottom, what he called 'points of maximum pessimism.'" This strategy made him a legend and earned him the title of "arguably the greatest global stock picker of the century" by *Money* Magazine. By 1992, Templeton's fund held more than $13 billion in assets, equivalent to $24.4 billion in today's value.

Fun Fact: When World War II broke out in 1939, Templeton borrowed money and bought more than 100 companies, 34 of which were in bankruptcy. The result? An estimated 400% return within 5 years.

Thomas Rowe Price, Jr.

anyone can do it ↓

1. "Change is the investor's only certainty."

2. "If you stay half-alert, you can pick the spectacular performers right from your place of business or out of the neighborhood shopping mall, and long before Wall Street discovers them."

3. "No one can see ahead 3 years, let alone 5 or 10. Competition, new inventions - all kinds of things - can change the situation in 12 months."

Investing Philosophy: T. Rowe Price gained fame for his "Growth Stock Investing Philosophy" of investing. He bought up-and-coming companies in early growth stages, making it a standard practice to interview a company's management before purchasing.

Fun Fact: Before becoming an investor, Thomas Rowe Price, Jr. was set to become a chemist.

Bill Ackman

1. "In order to be successful, you have to make sure that being rejected doesn't matter to you at all."

2. "Investing is a business where you can look very silly for a long time until you're proven right."

3. "Experience is making mistakes and learning from them."

Investing Philosophy: Bill Ackman, unlike the other investors on this list, added a proactive twist to value investing. Once he buys companies he believes are underpriced he pushes for change in the company. He can do this because he purchases massive amounts of stock until he owns enough that he's influential and important to the company. As a result, Ackman's portfolio averaged more than a 30% gain throughout 5 out of the last 16 years.

Fun Facts: Bill Ackman predicted the financial crisis in 2008, a feat that saved him millions and launched his status as a legendary investor.

Bill Miller

1. "Certainty belongs to mathematics, not to markets."

2. "We try to buy companies that trade at large discounts to intrinsic value. What's different is we will look for that value anywhere we can."

3. "If people are buying things they haven't analyzed ... it's not likely to end well." → do research

Investing Philosophy: Bill Miller, regarded as an investment genius as well as one of the top mutual fund managers of all time, has a few rules that keep him in the green. He doesn't try to predict where the market's going and instead looks for franchise value. He looks for new ideas and investments everywhere, but he doesn't often trade. The result? Miller's firm, called Miller Value Partners, posted a 119.5% net return in 2019 → why?

Fun Fact: Throughout the 2010s, Miller's firm once owned 12% of Facebook, 8% of Amazon and nearly 30% of Avon.

John Neff

1. "I don't want a lot of good investments; I want a few outstanding ones." → Quality winners

2. "Successful stocks don't tell you when to sell. When you feel like bragging it's probably time to sell."

3. "It's not always easy to do what's not popular, but that's where you make your money. Buy stocks that look bad to less careful investors and hang on until their real value is recognized."

Investing Philosophy: John Neff had a simple strategy: he believes in portfolio concentration as opposed to diversification and chooses stocks with a low P/E ratio in thriving industries. The fund Neff ran averaged a nearly 14% return throughout 30 years of investing.

Fun Fact: Neff believed that most people should invest 70% - 80% of their assets in equities, with most of that money being placed in, as stated above, good companies with low P/E ratios.

disagree

Jesse Livermore

1. "Money is made by sitting, not trading."

2. "The good speculators always wait and have patience, waiting for the market to confirm their judgment."

3. "Men (authors note: and women) who can both be right and sit tight are uncommon."

Investing Philosophy: Jesse Livermore, considered by many to be the most famous stock trader of all time, was a trend trader. He would buy strong and profitable stocks during bull markets and would short weak and losing stocks during bear markets. Like John Neff, Livermore leaned towards portfolio concentration as opposed to diversification. He purchased the best of the best and shorted the worst of the worst, no matter the diversification the strategy led to. As a result, Jesse Livermore made (in today's equivalent) more than $1 billion.

Fun Fact: The book *Reminiscences of a Stock Operator* by Edwin Lefevre is a fictionalized account of Livermore's rise to the stock trading elite. Despite being published in 1923, the book is still in print. It is one of the most widely known books on stock trading and in the words of William O'Neil (the founder of Investor's Business Daily), "in my 45 years of experience in this business, I have only found 10 or 12 books that were of any real value - *Reminiscences* is one of them."

Peter Lynch

1. "Never invest in any idea you can't illustrate with a crayon."

2. "Know what you own, and know why you own it."

3. "You don't need to be a rocket scientist. Investing is not a game where the guy with 160 IQ beats the guy with 130 IQ."

Investing Philosophy: Peter Lynch, an investing legend and author of a book that measures its sales in the millions, has a unique set of beliefs regarding stock trading. He believes that the individual investor has an advantage over professional traders because the individual investor has the ability to act quickly, isn't held back by legal means, and has so-called "local knowledge." The concept of "Trade what you know," as previously mentioned in this book, is largely based on Lynch's concepts. During his time as the head of Fidelity Magellan, he averaged a 29.2% return and grew the firm's assets from $20 million to $14 billion in 13 years.

Fun Fact: Lynch's best investment came from interacting with companies before those companies became great stocks. For example, Lynch was once on a trip to California when he happened to eat a really good burrito. As a result, he made millions off investing in Taco Bell. Since his retirement, Lynch has focused on humanitarian deeds, regarding them as a different form of investment. You can visit his charity at thelynchfoundation.com.

John C. "Jack" Bogle

1. "Learn every day, but especially from the experience of others. It's cheaper!"
2. "Time is your friend; impulse is your enemy."
3. "If you have trouble imagining a 20% loss in the stock market, you shouldn't be in stocks."

Investing Philosophy: Jack Bogle, founder of the Vanguard Group Inc., outlined 8 rules that sum up his investing philosophy in his book *Common Sense on Mutual Funds: New Imperatives for the Intelligent Investor*:

1. Select low-cost funds
2. Consider carefully the added costs of advice
3. Don't overrate past fund performance
1. Use past performance as a tool to determine risk
4. Beware of stars (stars meaning mutual fund managers)
5. Beware of asset size (large funds)
6. Own only a few funds
7. Buy and hold

Fun Fact: His investment management company, called The Vanguard Group, has $5.6 trillion in assets as of 2019. Yes, that's $5,600,000,000,000 in assets.

If it interests you, make sure to learn more about the fascinating lives of some of the greatest traders in history. Now, take a minute to write down a person who stuck with you, an idea that stuck with you, or anything else you would like to remember:

Buffet, Graham, Ackman, Livermore
lynch, Bogle — look into philosophies
& strategies more.

C

Conclusion: You Made It!

Congratulations. You have completed this book and being exposed to this information at an early age puts you in a very strong position. You have the opportunity to make more money than you or your parents have ever dreamed of as long as you put in the time and put in the work. Throughout this book, you have been introduced to making money, saving money, stock market literacy, stock market strategy, and the wisdom of the best investors of all time. However, although this book may be ending, your journey as an investor is just beginning. From now on, it's up to you.

Good luck.

Part VI: Resources and Further Information

This section will include a database of the best (not all of the best; new information is being released all the time) stock-related Websites, Books, TV shows, YouTube channels and Podcasts.

Websites:

- Investopedia.com (thanks Investopedia for reviewing this book!)
- Corporatefinanceinstitute.com
- Tradingview.com
- Stockrover.com
- Trendspider.com
- Metastock.com
- Yahoofinance.com
- Stockcharts.com
- Themotleyfool.com
- Metastock.com
- Morningstar.com
- Bloomberg.com
- Alphavantage.com
- Thewallstreetjournal.com
- Seekingalpha.com
- Zachs.com

Books:

Check your library before purchasing!

1. *One Up On Wall Street* by Peter Lynch (A personal favorite of mine)

2. *Get Rich Carefully* by Jim Cramer

3. *Mad Money: Watch TV, Get Rich* by Jim Cramer

4. *Stay Mad for Life: Get Rich, Stay Rich (Make Your Kids Even Richer)* by Jim Cramer

5. *Getting Back to Even* by Jim Cramer

6. *Real Money: Sane Investing in an Insane World* by Jim Cramer

7. *Confessions of a Street Addict* by Jim Cramer (This book is great as well as informative from a narrative stance)

8. *The Best Investment Advice I Ever Received: Priceless Wisdom from Warren Buffett, Jim Cramer, and Other Financial Experts* by Liz Claman

9. *You Got Screwed! Why Wall Street Tanked and How You Can Prosper* by Jim Cramer

10. *Pit Bull: Lessons From Wall Street's Champion Trader* by Martin "Buzzy" Schwartz

11. *The Daily Trading Coach: 101 Lessons for Becoming Your Own Trading Psychologist* by Brett N. Steenbarger

12. *How I Made $2 Million in the Stock Market: The Darvas System for Stock Market Profits* by Nicholas Darvas

13. *Trend Following: Learn to Make Millions in Up or Down Markets* by Michael W. Covel

14. *The Intelligent Investor: The Definitive Book on Value Investing* by Benjamin Graham

15. *Reminiscences of a Stock Operator* by Edwin Lefèvre

16. *The Automatic Millionaire* by David Bach

17. *The Wealthy Barber* by David Chilton

18. *The Man Who Beat the S&P: Investing with Bill Miller* by Janet Lowe

Robert Kiyosaki has written countless books on personal finance and investing. Here are a few must-reads from him, many of which are directed at teenagers.

PART VI: RESOURCES AND FURTHER INFORMATION

19. *Rich Dad Poor Dad* (A classic book that has sold more than 32 million copies)

20. *Wisdom from Rich Dad, Poor Dad for Teens: The Secrets about Money--That You Don't Learn in School!*

21. *Rich dad poor dad: What the rich teach their kids about money - That the poor and middle class do not!*

22. *Rich Kid Smart Kid: Giving Your Child a Financial Head Start*

23. *Rich Dad's Increase Your Financial IQ: Get Smarter with Your Money*

24. *Rich Dad's CASHFLOW Quadrant: Rich Dad's Guide to Financial Freedom*

25. *Rich dad poor dad: What the rich teach their kids about money - That the poor and middle class do not!*

26. *Rich Dad's Guide to Investing: What the Rich Invest in, That the Poor and Middle Class Do Not!*

TV Shows:

1. Mad Money™ from Jim Cramer (this show is great for a younger audience because its somewhat more entertaining than the others on this list).

2. Your Money™ from CNN

3. Squawk Box™ from CNBC

4. Money Matters™ from RLTV

YouTube Channels:

Financial Education -

https://www.youtube.com/financialeducation

Financial Education 2

https://www.youtube.com/channel/UCCmJVw9xQfYuuAAwZGedKR

Stock Market Investing -

https://www.youtube.com/channel/UC56LXfWGErp6D4XCnPP_soQ

*E*TRADE*

youtube.com/etrade

Learn To Invest

youtube.com/learntoinvest

The Monk Way - Stock Market Videos

youtube.com/themonkway

Podcasts:

1. Stacking Benjamins
2. Invest Like the Best
3. Money For The Rest Of Us
4. Money for the Rest of Us
5. Investing Insights from Morningstar
6. The College Investor
7. Invest Like a Boss
8. InvestTalk
9. Stacking Benjamins
10. Talking Wealth Podcast
11. The Investors Podcast
12. Sound Investing
13. Invest Like The Best
14. The Meb Faber Show
15. Best In Wealth Podcast
16. InPenny Stock
17. So Money
18. InvestED Podcast
19. We Study Billionaires
20. The BiggerPockets Money Podcast

Reselling Apps:

- Nextdoor
- Letgo
- OfferUp
- 5miles
- VarageSale
- Craigslist
- StockX
- Goat
- Grailed

Thank you for reading and thanks to all the amazing people who helped make this project happen. My goal is to educate, as was done to me, so if you're aware of a person who would perhaps benefit from a copy but can't afford it, or of an institution that might be interested in a copy, please reach out.

Now, in the words of Lucille Ball, go change the world!

©2021 Alan John

Sapere Aude

Printed in Great Britain
by Amazon